Decorating SCRAPBOOKS with *Rubber Stamps*

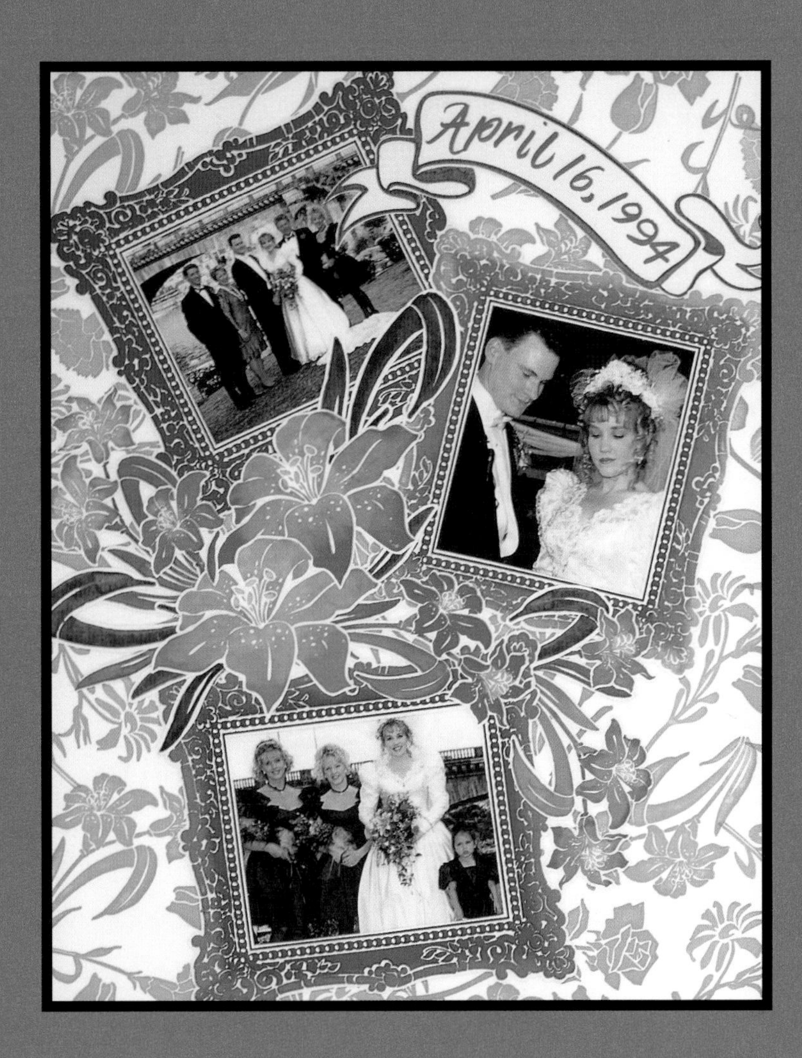

Sovereign of the Seas!

Decorating SCRAPBOOKS with *Rubber Stamps*

Dee Gruenig

Sterling Publishing Co., Inc. New York
A Sterling / Chapelle Book

Chapelle:
- Owner: Jo Packham
- Editor: Cathy Sexton
- Staff: Ann Bear, Areta Bingham, Kass Burchett, Rebecca Christensen, Leslie Farmer, Marilyn Goff, Shawn Hsu, Shirley Heslop, Holly Hollingsworth, Susan Jorgensen, Leslie Liechty, Pauline Locke, Ginger Mikkelsen, Barbara Milburn, Linda Orton, Karmen Quinney, Rhonda Rainey, and Cindy Stoeckl

Author's Note: A special thanks to the following people for their valuable assistance and loving support: Lynne Taylor, Vicki Sullivan, Shari Kowalke, Betty Waldeck, Jill Ham, Jill Cafferty, and, of course, my loving husband, Warren. I would also like to thank the following companies and manufacturers for providing materials that were used in this publication: Rubber Stampede, Marvy Uchida, Posh Impressions, Enchanted Creations, EK Success, Ivory Coast, Graven Images, Personal Stamp Exchange, Ranger Industries, Mrs. Grossman's Paper Company, All Night Media, Union Rubber, Burns & Allen, Savoir Faire, Fiskars, Family Treasures, C-Thru Ruler, Printworks, Mark Enterprises, Clearsnap, Evergreen, Yasutomo Co., Tsukineko, Inc., Paper Patch, and Hunt Manufacturing Co.

If you have any questions or comments or would like information on specialty products featured in this book, please contact Chapelle, Ltd., Inc., P.O. Box 9252, Ogden, UT 84409 • (801) 621-2777 • (801) 621-2788 Fax

If rubber cement is not available in your area, consult with any local crafts store to find a comparable product.

Library of Congress Cataloging-in-Publication Data

Gruenig, Dee.
Decorating scrapbooks with rubber stamps / Dee Gruenig.
p. cm.
"A Sterling / Chapelle book."
Includes index.
ISBN 0-8069-9841-5
1. Rubber stamp printing. 2. Scrapbooks. I. Title.
TT867.G76 1997
306.4—dc21 97-29479
CIP

A Sterling/Chapelle Book

10 9 8 7

First paperback edition published in 1999 by
Sterling Publishing Co., Inc.
387 Park Avenue South, New York, N.Y. 10016

Distributed in Canada by Sterling Publishing
℅ Canadian Manda Group, One Atlantic Avenue, Suite 105
Toronto, Ontario, Canada M6K 3E7
Distributed in Great Britain by Chrysalis Books Group PLC
The Chrysalis Building, Bramley Road, London W10 6SP, England
Distributed in Australia by Capricorn Link (Australia) Pty Ltd.
P.O. Box 704, Windsor, NSW 2756 Australia
Printed in China

Sterling ISBN 0-8069-9841-5 Trade
0-8069-9846-6 Paper

DEDICATION

This book is dedicated with love to the memory
of my father, Admiral Roy M. Davenport, U.S.N.

ABOUT THE AUTHOR

Scrapbooking has been a lifelong activity for Dee Gruenig. Influenced by her strict, but art-loving sixth grade teacher, Mrs. Azevedo, she became fascinated with making scrapbooks and journals, recording nearly everything around her. When first married, her husband Warren noticed that she always brought a camera to social events and outings, and that they had a bounty of memories to share with friends and family through photos.

It was a natural for Dee to introduce the creation of memory albums at her original rubber stamp and paper store in Southern California in 1986. She was truly the first to open customers' eyes to the endless possibilities using rubber stamps for memory making through her many workshops.

"From boring to beautiful" was her mission and it was really more of a total passion! Now she is sharing that passion for beauty and creativity through album art here as she has enthusiastically done all of her life.

Dee is well known to many as the dynamic featured presenter at many major events and also as an author, television personality, video instructor, and designer of the popular *Reflection Collection* "frame" stamps for photographs. These oversized stamps are quite possibly the first stamps to make a major impact on scrapbooks and memory albums, which are so popular today.

She earned her BA from Principia College with her major being education and a specialty in art history. Following, Dee attended Stanford University and received her Masters Degree in art education.

She still is majoring in art education, teaching what is possible to make lasting, meaningful, and memorable photo albums, scrapbooks, and journals at her two Posh Impressions store locations in Southern California.

CONTENTS

RUBBER STAMPS 8
STAMP PADS 8
MARKERS & PENS 8
BRAYERS & SPONGES 10
EMBOSSING POWDERS & HEAT TOOL 10
STICKER PAPERS 10
USING COLOR COPIED PHOTOS 10
USING STICKER PAPER FRAMES 11
SEVEN STEPS TO ALBUM ART SUCCESS 12
CREATING ALBUMS WITH THEMES 12
KEEPING A JOURNAL OF SPECIAL EVENTS 13
METRIC CONVERSION CHART 14
SIMPLY PAPER AND FRAMES 15
PEN STRIPE BACKGROUND 19
COMPRESSED SPONGE BACKGROUND 25
COPIED PAPER BACKGROUNDS 31
FABRIC COPIED BACKGROUND 35
BORDER STAMPING BACKGROUNDS 39
SHADES OF GRAY BACKGROUNDS 43
FULL PATTERN BACKGROUNDS 47
WHITE PATTERN BACKGROUNDS 51
STAMPED NEWSPAPER BACKGROUND 55
STAMPED LANDSCAPE BACKGROUNDS 59
WHITE EMBOSSED FRAMES 63
METALLIC EMBOSSED FRAMES 67
BRAYERED PEN DESIGNS 71
BRAYERED PLAID AND GINGHAMS 75
ENHANCED BRAYERED BACKGROUNDS 81
BRAYERED IMAGE BACKGROUNDS 85
BRAYERED LANDSCAPES 89
BRAYERED RAINBOW PAD BACKGROUND 93
BRAYERED RAINBOW PAD WITH SHADOWS AND HIGHLIGHTS 97
BRAYERED RAINBOW PAD RESIST BACKGROUNDS 101
SPONGE BRAYER WATERCOLOR BACKGROUNDS 105
BRAYERED REVERSE WITH SPATTERS 109
SPATTERED BACKGROUNDS 115
SPATTER BRUSH STREAKING BACKGROUNDS 119
GALLERY OF THEMED ALBUMS 123
INDEX 144

RUBBER STAMPS

Shown on page 9.

Artistic expression has exhibited itself since cave drawings. The creation of rubber stamps has brought art without anxiety and, because most of us still enjoy coloring, rubber stamping is a perfect art form.

To children, rubber stamps are toys or learning tools. To adults, they are practical, inexpensive, versatile implements for making things more colorful and personal.

Rubber stamps come in many shapes and sizes, and they are usually mounted on wood, foam, or on rollers. Rubber stamps bring color and creativity to a level that anyone can master!

HINTS:

- Use water-base markers. Colors can be blended right on the stamp.
- Coloring in two directions on large surfaces helps to insure against streaks or holes in the color.
- When using a large or very detailed stamp, if the ink has started to dry by the time you have finished coloring, it can be reactivated by exhaling on the stamp (like fogging a mirror). This technique is a good idea when using satin finish sticker paper since moist is a must!
- After coloring, press down firmly, making certain center and all edges have had pressure. Remember, the larger the stamp, the more pressure required. Lift stamp straight up off the paper without dragging it.
- Always have a stack of larger paper or a magazine under stamping projects to act as a cushion.

STAMP PADS

Shown on page 9.

One-color basic stamp pads with a felt surface are best used on outline design stamps which will be colored in with pens once the ink is dry. The ink is water-soluble and quick-drying.

Rainbow pads, of the hand-dyed variety, offer a fabulous blend of colors. Some of the dark colors used in rainbow pads tend to stain rubber stamps and brayers.

Pigment ink pads have an ingredient in them that makes the ink dry much slower. The colors in pigment-based rainbow pads will not blend with each other, so they stay perfectly separated. One of their biggest advantages is that the slow-drying inks allow time to add embossing powders that need to be heat-set. Pigment inks may be used without powders only on porous paper. If used on glossy paper without powder, they will never dry. Pigment pads come in many colors, including metallic, and are also available in white and in clear.

MARKERS & PENS

Shown on page 9.

Dual-tip water-base markers have a smaller size brush tip on one end and a fine writing tip on the other. Use the brush tip for coloring inside an outline type stamp design, or finer details on the rubber stamps. Use the fine tip for touch-ups and for writing or line accents.

Water-base felt brush-tip markers are the workhorses of color blending. The size of the brush tip applicator determines the speed of the color application.

White correction pens are used for white writing and for accenting. Use one specifically with a ball or roller-ball point applicator. The correction fluid dries quickly and has a wonderful opaque quality over dark backgrounds.

Permanent pigment ink pens are best for detailing, such as dots and "beeline" marks. They are also used for butterfly trails.

Scroll brush pens have a brush tip on one side and a double tip on the other. It is a split-edge calligraphy tip, slightly unequal, used for decorative bordering and creative line enhancements.

Water-base double-tip pens have a bullet tip on one end and a finer tip on the other. They give a nice variation of size, especially for "wallpaper-lined" backgrounds and for handwriting details.

Embossing pens come with various tips: fine, medium, wide, and calligraphy. They are filled with clear, slow-drying embossing ink. Embossing powder must be added to the ink and heated.

Calligraphy pens come in brilliant colors and double tips for multi-options. Different size lines are useful for writing as well as bordering enhancement and wide striped lines.

A
B
C

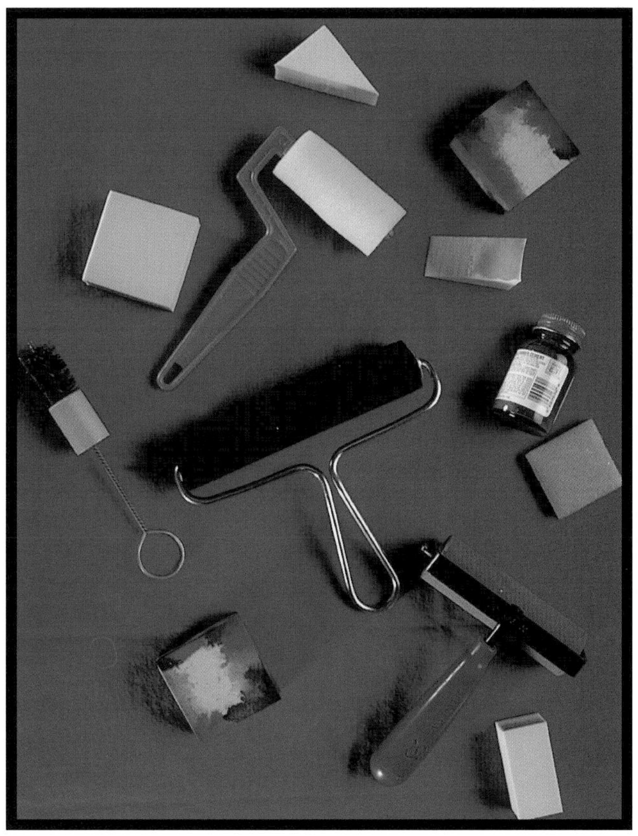

HINTS:

• Use a beveled ruler turned upside down to prevent the ink from getting on the ruler and being dragged across the paper when you move the ruler.

• Use fine- or medium-tip or calligraphy-tip water-base markers. Some permanent inks bleed or yellow with age. It is important to check for archival quality markers.

• Make lines evenly spaced. A light table with lined paper underneath can be helpful. Try vertical, diagonal, or two opposite directions for a plaid look.

• Hand drawn lines are a fun alternative. Do not use a ruler — lines do not always have to be perfect!

BRAYERS & SPONGES

Shown on page 9.

The soft rubber brayer is the most commonly used brayer for creating backgrounds. Brush markers can be used to color the soft rubber brayer. While the brayer is resting on its handle, apply the markers to the rubber roller as it is turned. Rubber brayers come in 2", 1", and 6" widths.

The black foam brayer is made from a hard-textured sponge-type material, and because of its texture, a softer look is rendered. Ink the entire surface of the brayer by rolling it over hand-dyed rainbow pads. Brush markers can also be used to color the black foam brayer, but it is difficult to see the ink on the dark surface.

The sponge brayer is made of a soft sponge material and has a plastic handle. These brayers are very inexpensive. Use brush markers to color the surface of the brayer in random patterns; then spray it with a light mist of water. Roll it over a stamping surface to create a watercolor background.

Good-quality wedge-shaped makeup sponges can be used with brush art markers to create several effects. Color one end of the sponge, and blot lightly to test the color intensity. Dabbing the sponge around the edge of the artwork gives a soft air-brushed look. Dab over and over without blotting for darker colors.

A compressed sponge starts out as a large sponge, but is compressed down to about 2" x 2" x 1". Because of its density, it holds a lot of ink and is great for making streaked patterns. Compressed sponges are much harder than makeup sponges.

EMBOSSING POWDERS & HEAT TOOL

Embossing powders are available in many opaque colors, as well as metallic, irridescent, and sparklers, which contain glitter. These powders are poured over pigment inks. The excess should be shaken off, and the powder is then set using a heat tool.

Heat tools are made for embossing. They get very hot, but they do not blow much air. Therefore a hair dryer will not work.

STICKER PAPERS

Shown on page 9.

There are two photo safe sticker papers available.

One is glossy and practically foolproof for stamping quality. However, it does not have a crack and peel backing so it is sometimes difficult to separate. Start at a corner and roll your thumb over the edge to separate the layers or push your fingernail between them to get started. Peel away only a small portion until the placement has been determined.

The second choice is satin finish opaque. This requires juicy brush art markers to get a good solid stamped image since the ink soaks into the paper, but because of its opacity, the background will not show through. This sticker paper has a crack and peel backing and is therefore very easy to remove. This sticker paper is the best choice for light colored stickers that will be placed on dark or busy backgrounds and also for journaling stamps with large negative areas.

USING COLOR COPIED PHOTOS

It is recommended that a color copy of all photos be used. Originals should always be kept in a safe environment in case duplicates should ever need to be made.

Color copies work well because they do not fade like original photos and they are thinner which makes it easier when layering with frames and mats.

Copies can be reduced or enlarged as desired, therefore making any size photo possible to accommodate any page layout idea and any frame.

Photos are not the only items that can be color copied. Using a rubber stamp, stamp an image onto any piece of paper. Color copy the image in a reduced or enlarged format and use several images of the same size or various sizes.

To add interest to any page, a silhouette can be made by cutting the image out of the photo. When doing this, cut the image very close to the edge. When placing these images on the background paper, make certain to glue the edges securely if they meet the edge of the page.

Spray adhesive can be used and gives a wonderful bond but it is not acid free, therefore other options might be preferred.

USING STICKER PAPER FRAMES

Use a sharp craft knife to begin cutting the center from any stamped frame. Once it is started, sharp craft scissors can be inserted to finish.

Place the photo behind the opening of the stamped frame. Hold it firmly in position and cut the photo in from the edges of the frame. If necessary, trim more so there will be some sticky backing around all edges.

Peel away just one edge or corner of the backing. Line up the photo in the opening. Check the placement before removing the remaining backing and carefully remove the photo if it needs adjusting.

Place the frame right side down and peel away one side of the backing at a time. Keep the frame flat before pressing down the photo. Repeat for the remaining sides.

Carefully place the framed photo into position on the background paper. Start with one corner and smooth it out gradually.

It is sometimes helpful to reattach the backing until you are certain of the exact placement. This allows the position to be changed if you change your mind.

When cutting around stamped images, it is best to leave a tiny white border. This keeps you from cutting into the design and enhances the white details in the design. It also gives a larger, easier to handle area when cutting words or small images.

SEVEN STEPS TO ALBUM ART SUCCESS

1. CHOOSING PHOTOS

Naturally, this step begins with taking the photos. Think about the photos telling a story, and as in any story, not all the photos have to be of a group or individual. Take supporting photos of signs and locations.

Then when it is time to go through the photos, it will be easy to coordinate the theme for each page and decide which photos relate best with each other.

2. SIZING PHOTOS

For variety, it is important not to keep all your photos the same size and shape. Color copies are wonderful because the size of each photo can be varied. Enlarge focal points for silhouetting and reduce photos to fit virtually any stamped image. The other advantage to color copying your photos is that is allows the use of the original photo many times in many different ways.

3. SELECTING PAPERS

Once a photo and general theme has been chosen to use on a given album page, it is necessary to coordinate with paper backgrounds. Colorful matts for photos should also be selected at this time.

4. MATTING AND FRAMING PHOTOS

Next, pull together the rubber stamps that relate to or coordinate with the photos and papers you want to use.

For your stamped images, you will need to use brush art markers in coordinating colors to color the rubber stamps. Stamp the image(s) onto acid free sticker paper. It is easiest to stamp all of the necessary images at one time, as you can fit quite a few on one page. Once the ink has dried, cut the images out with scissors. Use a sharp craft knife to cut out the insides of the photo frames.

Do not limit yourself to one single color mat. You can double or triple mat each photo using a variety of papers and paper edgers.

5. ARRANGING PAGES

Place the photos with their stamped frames and mats in a variety of arrangements until you find one that is perfect.

At this time, enhance the page by adding additional rubber stamped images.

To secure everything, use an acid free adhesive or remove the backing from the sticker paper and place the photos and stamped images into position.

6. JOURNALING

This step truly ties the album page together and gives meaning to those who are seeing it.

Journaling looks wonderful inside a rubber stamped image such as the banner. The information can vary from a basic name or title to more information about the photos and people involved.

Brush art markers can be used on rubber stamp alphabet sets or stylized writing can be done with any acid free pen.

7. PROTECTING THE FINISHED PAGES

The most common way to protect the finished pages is simply to slip the completed pages into acid free sheet protectors and place the pages into a three-ring binder.

Another alternative is to laminate the pages with acid free lamination. This option allows for more choices as you can use a variety of different sized albums. Simply punch holes in the pages to coordinate with the structure of the album.

CREATING ALBUMS WITH THEMES

Shown on pages 123-143.

When putting albums together, remember that it is not necessary to start at the beginning of time and continue adding, chronologically, forever.

Divide your albums into smaller, more interesting albums that carry specific themes.

Album themes can vary from the first year of a child's life, to a favorite family vacation, to an album filled with photos of family pets, to documentation of a special season or event. The photo gallery in this book will give fun ideas that might help you categorize your photos.

The most important thing to remember when working with a chosen theme is to coordinate the entire album, including the cover, in some way. The cover must be inviting so that others will want to open it up and see what's inside.

KEEPING A JOURNAL OF SPECIAL EVENTS

Shown here and on page 140.

Keeping a journal can be just as important as taking photos.

When was the last time you could remember every detail of a special event? That is why journaling is so important — it helps document things that might otherwise soon be forgotten.

Take time to write down all the wonderful experiences or memories of special events. That way, whenever you are ready to create your album, you have a script to follow. You can even incorporate journal pages into your album as shown on page 140.

Let's say it is a special vacation that you want to document. Before you depart on your journey, take the time to find a mini journal that is easy to carry with you at all times.

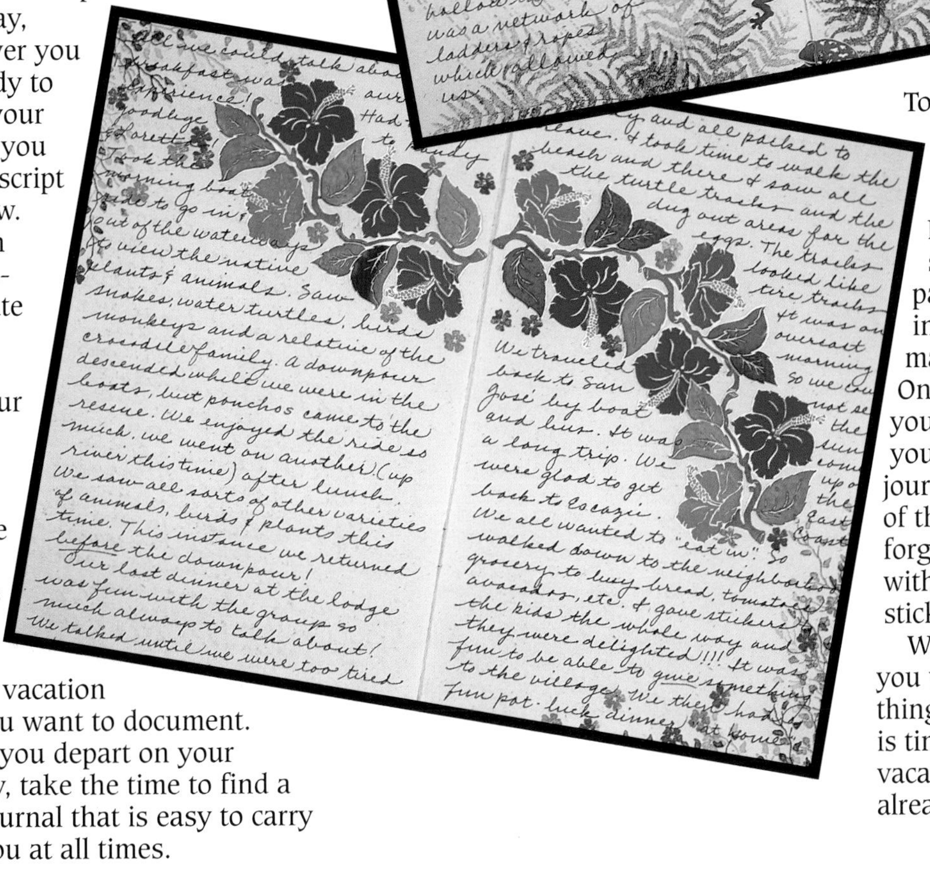

To customize the journal, stamp some general background designs on some of the inside pages. In addition, stamp several images on sticker paper. These stamped images can be cut out to make stickers.

Once you have arrived at your vacation destination, you are ready to begin journaling. As you take note of things you won't want to forget, embellish the pages with the stamped image stickers.

When your vacation is over, you will have captured everything in writing so that when it is time to begin creating the vacation album, half the work is already done.

METRIC CONVERSION CHART

INCHES	MM	CM
1/8	3	0.9
1/4	6	0.6
3/8	10	1.0
1/2	13	1.3
5/8	16	1.6
3/4	19	1.9
7/8	22	2.2
1	25	2.5

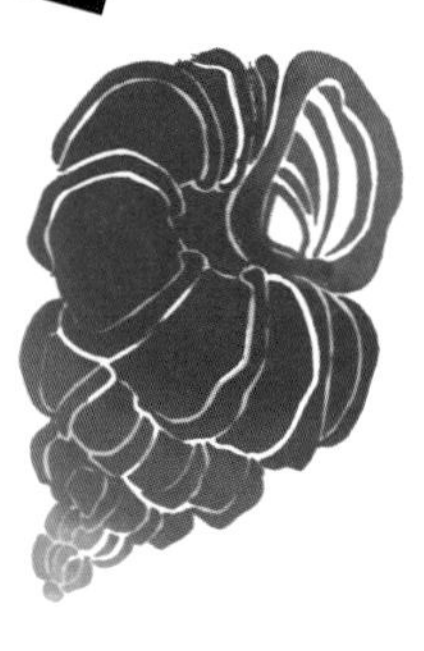

Simply Paper and Frames

To begin designing an album, background paper is chosen that reflects a desired look that will be carried throughout the entire album. Whether the album is to be bright and colorful, soft and elegant, simple, or sophisticated, the choice of color and texture of the background paper is an important first step.

Photo frames accentuate photos and are an integral element when designing pages. Photo frames can be cut apart to make frames that are custom sized. In addition, photo frames can be made from "clustering" a series of stickers made from stamping images on sticker paper and then cutting them out.

CARIBBEAN FUN

Shown on page 15.

Create this page on a background paper of white with small confetti flecks.

Using rubber stamps, stamp all rope frames and seashells on sticker paper.

Trim photos to fit into stamped frames and cut out all stamped images to make stickers.

Lay-out the page and carefully adhere all photos and stamped image stickers into position on the background paper.

Stamp confetti dots randomly around the page.

LITTLE ARTIST

Shown on page 17.

Create this page on a background paper of black linen.

Using rubber stamps, stamp paintbrushes, bow, easel, paint palette, and banner on sticker paper.

Using deckled paper edgers, cut a white mat for top photo. Adhere cut mat on red paper and trim to a 1/4" mat. Trim top photo to fit on white mat and silhouette remaining photo.

Cut out all stamped images to make stickers. Cut out paint blobs from colored paper.

Lay-out the page and carefully adhere all photos, stamped image stickers, and paint blobs into position on the background paper.

CAMELOT WEDDING

Shown on page 18.

Create these pages on background paper with a soft green marble print.

Using rubber stamps, stamp all four rope frames, ribbons and bows, and several clusters of roses on sticker paper. Stamp the banners on tan paper.

Using a colored marker, write the names of the bride and groom on one banner and the wedding date on the remaining banner.

Trim photos to fit into stamped frames and cut out all stamped images to make stickers.

Lay-out the pages and carefully adhere all photos and stamped image stickers into position on the background paper.

COSTA RICA

Shown on page 18.

Create these pages on background paper of white with small confetti flecks.

Using rubber stamps, stamp eight twisted leaf frames, banner, sun, and several different flowers on sticker paper.

Using a colored marker, write the desired phrase on the banner.

Trim photos to fit into stamped frames and cut out all stamped images to make stickers.

Lay-out the pages and carefully adhere all photos and stamped image stickers into position on the background paper.

ARTIST...
JUST FOR MOMMY

Lana and Mark
October 10, 1992
Costa Rica

MC KYE!

Pen Stripe Background

To create striped backgrounds, a beveled ruler, turned upside down, is used for making straight lines across a page. Turning the ruler upside down prevents ink from getting on the ruler and being dragged across the paper.

It is important to make lines evenly spaced. Using a light table with ruled paper underneath the page can be helpful.

Try lines that are vertical, horizontal, or diagonal. Two lines drawn in opposite directions give a plaid look. Hand-drawn lines, made without a ruler, can be a fun alternative.

Use a water-based or pigment ink marker for drawing all lines. Permanent ink sometimes bleeds or yellows over time, so check for archival quality.

SUNFLOWER BABY

Shown on page 19.

Create this page on a background paper of solid white.

Using colored markers, create the background design by making fine diagonal lines about 1/4" apart.

Using rubber stamps, stamp banner and several sunflowers on sticker paper.

Using colored markers, write the desired phrase on the banner.

Trim photos as desired. Adhere photos on coordinating colors of paper and trim to a 1/4" mat.

Cut out all stamped images to make stickers.

Lay-out the page and carefully adhere all photos and stamped image stickers into position on the background paper.

PANSY PORTRAIT

Shown on page 21.

Create this page on a background paper of solid white.

Using a blue marker, create the background design by making fine double diagonal lines in two directions about 1" apart.

Using rubber stamps, stamp bow, tag, and several pansies on sticker paper.

Using colored markers, write the desired phrase on the tag.

Trim the photo in an oval shape and cut out all stamped images to make stickers.

Lay-out the page and carefully adhere photo and all stamped image stickers into position on the background paper. Overlap pansies as desired to make a natural looking border around the photo.

PLAYER OF THE GAME

Shown on page 23.

Create this page on a background paper of solid white.

Using a black marker, create the background design by making fine vertical lines about 1/8" apart.

Using rubber stamps, stamp billboard frame, newspaper frame, bulletin board, banner, both flags, baseballs and bats, and grass with flowers on sticker paper.

Using colored markers, write the desired headline on newspaper frame and the desired captions on bulletin board and banner.

Trim photos to fit into stamped frames and cut out all stamped images to make stickers. If desired, silhouette one photo.

Lay-out the page and carefully adhere all photos and stamped image stickers into position on the background paper.

Using a red marker, create the "bounce" pattern of the baseballs.

FUTURE BASEBALL STARS

Shown on page 23.

Create this page on a background paper of solid red.

Using a white ballpoint correction pen, create the background design by making fine double vertical lines about 1/2" apart.

Using rubber stamps, stamp both star frames, award ribbon, and additional stars on sticker paper.

Using a black marker, write the desired phrase in the center of the award ribbon.

Our Sweet Boy!

Adhere one photo on white paper and trim to a 1/4" mat, then place cut mat on top of blue paper. Using jigsaw paper edgers, trim blue mat.

Trim photos to fit into stamped frames and cut out all stamped images to make stickers. If desired, silhouette one photo.

Lay-out the page and carefully adhere all photos and stamped image stickers into position on the background paper.

WELCOME TO NEW MEXICO

Shown on page 23.

Create this page on a background paper of solid white.

Using dark blue and light blue markers, create the background design by hand-drawing fine double horizontal and vertical lines about 1/2" apart. At each intersection, make a small dark blue square.

Using rubber stamps, stamp window frame, billboard frame, car, and a rocky road on sticker paper.

Stamp or write the desired phrase on the billboard frame.

Using a blue marker, personalize the license plate on the car.

Trim one photo to fit into stamped frame. Trim two photos as desired. Adhere on blue paper and trim to a 1/4" mat. If desired, silhouette one or more photos.

Cut out all stamped images to make stickers.

Lay-out the page and carefully adhere all photos and stamped image stickers into position on the background paper.

HOWDY PARTNER

Shown on page 23.

Create this page on a background paper of solid white.

Using a blue marker, create the background design by making fine double vertical lines about 1/2" apart.

Using rubber stamps, stamp bandana, lasso, photo corners, and "HAD A GREAT TIME" on sticker paper.

Stamp or write "HOWDY" in the center of the lasso.

Trim photos as desired and cut out all stamped images to make stickers.

Lay-out the page and carefully adhere all photos and stamped image stickers into position on the background paper.

ENGINE ENGINE NUMBER NINE

Shown on page 24.

Create this page on a background paper of solid white.

Using a black marker, create the background design by making fine double horizontal and vertical lines about 1/4" apart.

Cut an oval train track from black paper. Using a white ballpoint correction pen, draw the track lines on the track.

Using rubber stamps, stamp two rows of houses and one admission ticket on sticker paper.

Stamp or write the desired phrase in the center of the admission ticket.

Trim photos as desired. Adhere photos on red paper and trim to a 1/4" mat. If desired, silhouette one or more photos.

Cut out all stamped images to make stickers.

Lay-out the page and carefully adhere all photos and stamped image stickers into position on the background paper.

WHITE SOX
SCHEDULE:
* GAME ON
TUESDAY
DAILY TIMES 25¢
PLAYER OF THE GAME
JAKE

FUTURE
BASEBALL
STARS

WELCOME
TO NEW
MEXICO
TRVLN

Had a
GREAT
Time
Howdy

ADMIT ONE
TRAIN RIDE 25¢
ADMIT ONE
THE END
THE END

Compressed Sponge Background

Compressed sponges are very dense and therefore can hold a lot of ink. Using brush art markers, color both sides of one edge of the sponge with several colors as shown in the photos on page 14. Spray the sponge with a light mist of water and pull the sponge across the page, starting and ending off the edge for a continuous flow of color. Repeat and re-ink sponge as necessary.

Try diagonal and curved lines and, for a plaid look, sponge lines in opposite directions.

When the sponge is thoroughly dry, another edge can be used for another color combination. Compressed sponges can be washed out, but the colors will stain. It is best to designate several sponges for several different color combinations and never use a sponge stained with dark colors for lighter combinations.

Before adding images to the page, allow it to thoroughly dry.

Sri Lanka

SRI LANKA

Shown on page 25.

Create this page on a background paper of solid white.

Using a compressed sponge, create the background design by making wavy stripes with gray, beige, and ochre.

Using rubber stamps, stamp twisted leaf frames, banner, and several palm trees on sticker paper.

Using a colored marker, write the desired phrase on the banner.

Trim photos to fit into stamped frames and cut out all stamped images to make stickers.

Lay-out the page and carefully adhere all photos and stamped image stickers into position on the background paper.

SUDAN

Shown on page 27.

Create this page on a background paper of solid white.

Using a compressed sponge, create the background design by making diagonal stripes with shades of blue and aqua.

Using rubber stamps, stamp brick frames, rocks, banner, and sun on sticker paper.

Using a colored marker, write the desired phrase on the banner.

Trim photos to fit into stamped frames. Trim two photos as desired. Adhere photos on blue paper and trim to a $^{1}/_{4}$" mat.

Cut out all stamped images to make stickers.

Lay-out the page and carefully adhere all photos and stamped image stickers into position on the background paper.

ALOHA!

Shown on page 29.

Create this page on a background paper of solid white.

Using a compressed sponge, create the background design by making curved stripes with yellow, pink, fuschia, blue, and green.

Using rubber stamps, stamp both tags and several flowers on sticker paper.

Stamp or write the word "ALOHA," or use a desired word or phrase, on sticker paper.

Using colored markers, write the desired phrases on the tags.

Trim photos as desired. Adhere photos on coordinating colors of paper and trim to a minimum 1" mat.

Cut out all stamped images to make stickers.

Using the stamped flower stickers, make frames around the photos. Overlap flowers as desired to make a natural looking border. Trim around photo frames along the contour of the flower border to a $^{1}/_{4}$" mat.

Lay-out the page and carefully adhere all photos and stamped image stickers into position on the background paper.

PLAYGROUND PASTIME

Shown on page 29.

Create this page on a background paper of solid white.

Sudan

Using a compressed sponge, create the background design by making a horizontal and vertical plaid with yellow, pink, fuschia, blue, and green.

Using rubber stamps, stamp twig frames and arrow sign on sticker paper. Stamp leaves with flowers around corners of the twig frames.

Lightly sponge over leaves and flowers with light green to blend them into the background.

Stamp or write the desired phrase on the arrow sign.

Trim photos to fit into stamped frames and cut out all stamped images to make stickers.

Lay-out the page and carefully adhere all photos and stamped image stickers into position on the background paper.

MY BABY BOY

Shown on page 29.

Create this page on a background paper of solid white.

Using a compressed sponge, create the background design by making opposite diagonal stripes with aqua, turquoise, and blue.

Using rubber stamps, stamp ribbon frames and locket on sticker paper.

Stamp and emboss all bandanas with white on turquoise paper.

Stamp or write the desired phrase in the center of the locket.

Trim photos to fit into stamped frames and cut out all stamped images to make stickers. Trim one photo to fit inside the remaining side of locket.

Lay-out the page and carefully adhere all photos and stamped image stickers into position on the background paper.

UNDER THE SEA

Shown on page 29.

Create this page on a background paper of solid white.

Using a compressed sponge, create the background design by making wavy diagonal stripes with shades of blue and aqua.

Using rubber stamps, stamp twisted leaf frames, banner, and several fish on sticker paper.

Using a colored marker, write the desired phrase on the banner.

Trim photos to fit into stamped frames and cut out all stamped images to make stickers.

Lay-out the page and carefully adhere all photos and stamped image stickers into position on the background paper.

SET SAIL FROM AMERICA

Shown on page 30.

Create this page on a background paper of solid white.

Using a compressed sponge, create the background design by making diagonal stripes with two shades of red and two shades of blue.

Using rubber stamps, stamp flags, anchors, and banner on sticker paper.

Stamp and emboss rope frames with white on red and blue paper.

Using a colored marker, write the desired phrase on the banner.

Trim photos to fit into stamped frames and cut out all stamped images to make stickers.

Lay-out the page and carefully adhere all photos and stamped image stickers into position on the background paper.

Aloha!
Layla "n" Nathan
Kara "n" Layla
KARA
NATHAN
MY BABY BOY
"LAYLA"

BON & DICK SET
SAIL FROM AMERICA!

Copied Paper Backgrounds

When designing an album, sometimes the perfect background paper is something that is not practical.

This chapter includes some clever ideas for making background paper out of some of those impractical things, such as heavily textured paper, sheer paper, book pages, cardboard, and even a map. Simply color copy any of these items and you instantly have a full color background paper that is unique and is the perfect selection for the theme being portrayed.

EGYPT

EGYPT

Shown on page 31.

Make a color copy of a map to create a background paper — it is best to use a map from the part of the world that is being depicted. Any map will do, because much of it will be covered.

Using rubber stamps, stamp film roll frame, camera frame, banner, and push pins on sticker paper.

Using colored markers, write the desired phrase on the banner.

Trim photos to fit into stamped frames and cut out all stamped images to make stickers. If desired, silhouette one photo.

Lay-out the page and carefully adhere all photos and stamped image stickers into position on the background paper.

Using a gray marker, make a shadow on the left sides and bottoms of the photos that are not inside stamped frames. Make a shadow around the banner.

ALVA LOUISE

Shown on page 33.

Place a doily on a piece of gray paper and make a color copy of it to create a background paper.

Using rubber stamps, stamp several roses and a banner on sticker paper.

Using a black marker, write the desired phrase on the banner.

Trim the photo to fit in the center of the doily and cut out all stamped images to make stickers.

Lay-out the page and carefully adhere photo and stamped image stickers into position on the background paper.

DEE & WARREN

Shown on page 34.

Make copies of pages from the Bible to create background paper — use pages from the Bible that have verses with special significance. Make a reduced color copy of the Bible's cover.

Using rubber stamps, stamp and emboss a banner with gold on white paper. Stamp and emboss several roses with metallic colors on black paper.

Using a black marker, write the desired phrase on the banner.

Trim photos as desired and cut around the color copy of the Bible's cover. Adhere two photos on gold paper and trim to a 1/4" mat. Place the copy of the Bible's cover on gold paper and trim to resemble a book.

Cut out all stamped images to make stickers.

Lay-out the pages and carefully adhere all photos and stamped image stickers into position on the background paper.

MACHU PICCHU

Shown on page 34.

Make copies of heavily textured paper to create background paper.

Using rubber stamps, stamp all five brick frames, photo corners, pottery, scroll, wildflowers, and leaves on sticker paper.

Using a colored marker, write the desired caption on the scroll.

Trim photos to fit into stamped frames and cut out all stamped images to make stickers.

Lay-out the pages and carefully adhere all photos and stamped image stickers into position on the background paper.

Alva Louise

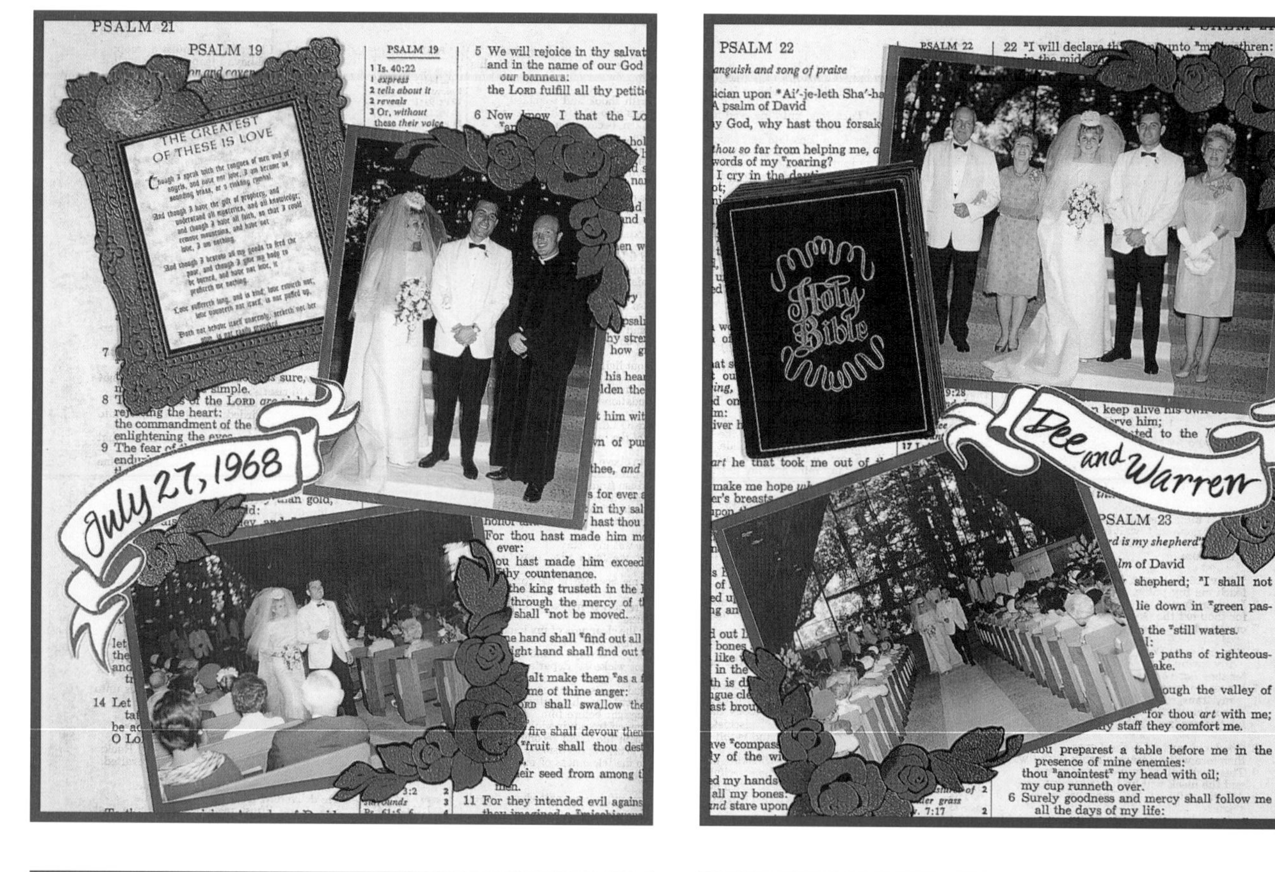
THE GREATEST OF THESE IS LOVE
July 27, 1968
Holy Bible
Dee and Warren
PSALM 19
PSALM 22
PSALM 23

In all our travels Machu Picchu, lost city of the Incas, will stand out as the most inspirational!

Fabric-Copied Background

As in the previous chapter, this chapter includes some clever ideas for making custom background paper. Simply color copy any fabric and, if necessary, trim it down to the desired size.

HAITI

Shown on page 35.

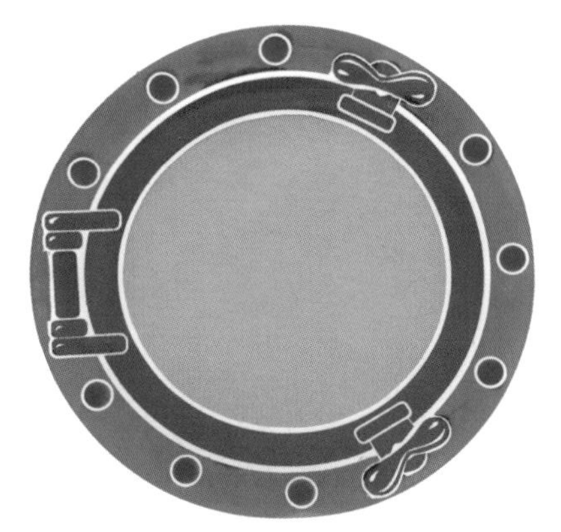

Make a color copy of tropical-print fabric to create a background paper.

Using rubber stamps, stamp two banners on sticker paper.

Stamp and emboss four porthole frames with white on red paper.

Stamp or write the desired phrases on the banners.

Trim photos to fit into stamped frames and cut out all stamped images to make stickers.

Punch out holes in porthole frames so background paper shows through.

Lay-out the page and carefully adhere all photos and stamped image stickers into position on the background paper.

FABULOUS FRIENDS

Shown on page 37.

Make a color copy of stonewashed denim fabric to create a background paper.

Using rubber stamps, stamp three rope frames, two bandanas, lasso, and banner on sticker paper. Remove the center section of two rope frames and use it to make the fourth frame.

Using a colored marker, write the desired phrases in the center of the lasso and on the banner.

Trim photos to fit into stamped frames and cut out all stamped images to make stickers.

Punch several small stars out of white paper.

Lay-out the page and carefully adhere all photos and stamped image stickers into position on the background paper.

HONG KONG

Shown on page 38.

Make a color copy of Oriental-print brocade fabric to create background paper.

Using rubber stamps, stamp several flowers and a banner on sticker paper.

Stamp and emboss six bamboo frames with white on turquoise paper. Make one large frame from two stamped frames.

Stamp or write the desired phrase on the banner.

Trim photos to fit into stamped frames and cut out all stamped images to make stickers. If desired, silhouette one photo for the bottom of each page — use landscape or skyline photos for an impressive way to add dimension.

Lay-out the pages and carefully adhere all photos and stamped image stickers into position on the background paper.

ITALIAN GOURMET

Shown on page 38.

Make a color copy of red gingham fabric topped with uncooked linguini noodles to create background paper.

Using rubber stamps, stamp carnations, banner, and jar on sticker paper.

Stamp and emboss six raffia frames with white and ochre on black paper. Make one large frame from two stamped frames.

Using a colored marker, write the desired phrase on the banner. Stamp "MENU" in the top area of the jar. Write the desired menu inside the jar underneath the stamped area.

Trim photos to fit into stamped frames and cut out all stamped images to make stickers. If desired, silhouette one or more photos.

Lay-out the pages and carefully adhere all photos and stamped image stickers into position on the background paper.

Rankin
Ranch
1994
FABULOUS
FRIENDS & FAMILY

HONG KONG

Menu
1. Pasta
2. Pasta
3. Pasta
4. Wine

Italian Gourmet

Border Stamping Backgrounds

For times when a full patterned background is too much, border stamping is the perfect solution. Choose a rubber stamp that coordinates with the entire page layout. Color stamp with brush art markers and stamp around the entire edge of the paper. If the stamp design allows, stamp off the page. One to $1^1/_2$" borders work best.

VACATION FUN

Shown on page 39.

Using rubber stamps, stamp squares in a checkerboard pattern around the entire outside edge of cream speckled paper to make a border.

Stamp photo corners, chili peppers, and scroll on sticker paper.

Using a black marker, write the desired phrase in the center of the scroll.

Trim photos as desired and cut out all stamped images to make stickers.

Lay-out the page and carefully adhere all photos and stamped image stickers into position on the background paper.

BIG CHIEF

Shown on page 41.

Using rubber stamps, stamp photo corners around the entire outside edge of brown kraft paper to make a border.

Stamp photo corners, snakes, and sign on sticker paper.

Using a black marker, write the desired phrase on the sign.

Trim photos as desired. Adhere photos on black paper and trim to a 1/8" mat.

Cut out all stamped images to make stickers.

Lay-out the page and carefully adhere all photos and stamped image stickers into position on the background paper.

DOUG & CAREY

Shown on page 42.

Using rubber stamps, stamp small flowers and dots around the entire outside edge of white glossy paper to make a border.

Stamp oval frames and banner on sticker paper.

Using colored markers, write the desired phrase on the banner.

Trim photos to fit into stamped frames and cut out all stamped images to make stickers.

Lay-out the page and carefully adhere all photos and stamped image stickers into position on the background paper.

CANNON'S CHRISTMAS

Shown on page 42.

Using rubber stamps, stamp evergreen sprigs around the entire outside edge of white glossy paper to make a border. Randomly stamp small dots.

Stamp ornament frames, gift box, and ribbons on sticker paper.

Using a colored marker, write the desired phrase in the center of one ornament frame.

Trim two photos to fit into stamped frames. Trim remaining photos as desired. Adhere on coordinating colors of paper and trim to a 1/4" mat. If desired, silhouette one photo.

Cut out all stamped images to make stickers.

Lay-out the page and carefully adhere all photos and stamped image stickers into position on the background paper.

SAILING AWAY

Shown on page 42.

Using rubber stamps, stamp wavy blocks around the entire outside edge of white glossy paper to make a border.

Stamp three rope frames and banner on sticker paper.

Using a colored marker, write the desired phrase on the banner.

Trim photos to fit into stamped frames and cut out all stamped images to make stickers.

Lay-out the page and carefully adhere all photos and stamped image stickers into position on the background paper.

MICHAEL

Shown on page 42.

Using rubber stamps, stamp brush strokes around the entire outside edge of white glossy paper to make a border.

Stamp photo corners and banner on sticker paper.

Stamp or write the desired phrase on the banner.

Trim photos as desired and cut out all stamped images to make stickers.

Lay-out the page and carefully adhere all photos and stamped image stickers into position on the background paper.

BIG
CHIEF
LITTLE
BRAVE

Doug Carey
Cannon's Christmas 1996
Sailing Away!
MICHAEL

Shades of Gray Backgrounds

Background paper made with shades of gray is a favorite because of the interesting contrast of colors.

Begin with a white glossy paper and ink the stamp with a medium gray color brush art marker. In a free form or repeated pattern, stamp it several times until the entire background paper is covered. It is important to stamp off the edge of the paper to give a completed look.

Keep the same stamp handy as it may add to the album page design stamped in contrasting colors.

SEA WORLD

Shown on page 43.

Stamp or write the word "MEMORIES," or use a desired word or phrase, in a wave-like pattern over the entire surface of white glossy paper to create a background.

Using rubber stamps, stamp porthole frames, bubbles, and banner on sticker paper.

Using a colored marker, write the desired phrase on the banner.

Trim photos to fit into stamped frames and cut out all stamped images to make stickers. If desired, silhouette one or more photos.

Lay-out the page and carefully adhere all photos and stamped image stickers into position on the background paper.

EAT YOUR VEGGIES

Shown on page 45.

Using rubber stamps, stamp a variety of vegetables over the entire surface of white glossy paper to create a background.

Stamp twig frames and additional vegetables on sticker paper.

Trim photos to fit into stamped frames and cut out all stamped images to make stickers.

Lay-out the page and carefully adhere all photos and stamped image stickers into position on the background paper.

BEACH COMBING

Shown on page 46.

Using rubber stamps, stamp a variety of seashells over the entire surface of white glossy paper to create a background.

Stamp and emboss rope frames with white on gray paper.

Stamp banner and additional seashells on sticker paper.

Using a colored marker, write the desired phrase on the banner.

Trim photos to fit into stamped frames and cut out all stamped images to make stickers.

Lay-out the page and carefully adhere all photos and stamped image stickers into position on the background paper.

SPRING WEDDING

Shown on page 1.

Using rubber stamps, stamp a variety of flowers over the entire surface of white glossy paper to create a background.

Stamp ornate frames, several large and small lillies, and banner on sticker paper.

Using a colored marker, write the desired phrase on the banner.

Trim photos to fit into stamped frames and cut out all stamped images to make stickers.

Lay-out the page and carefully adhere all photos and stamped image stickers into position on the background paper.

Beach Combing

This fun, yet very customized stamped background, allows the perfect background paper to be created.

Once a theme has been chosen, choose a rubber stamp that will make a strong background. A key to choosing the right rubber stamp is focusing on a design or pattern stamp, usually on the smaller side.

Color the stamp with brush art markers, remembering not to limit yourself to one color. In a free form pattern, stamp it several times until the entire background paper is covered. It is important to stamp off the edge of the paper to give a completed look.

White glossy paper works best for these full pattern backgrounds.

Full Pattern Backgrounds

LUAU LAUGHTER

Shown on page 47.

Using rubber stamps, stamp small free-form flowers randomly over the entire surface of white glossy paper to create a background.

Stamp several large flowers on sticker paper.

Trim photos as desired. Adhere photos on coordinating colors of paper and trim to a $^1/_4$" mat.

Cut out all stamped images to make stickers.

Lay-out the page and carefully adhere all photos and stamped image stickers into position on the background paper.

JAKE'S & COLBY'S GARDEN

Shown on page 49.

Using rubber stamps, stamp small dots randomly over the entire surface of white glossy paper to create a background.

Stamp seed packet frames, butterflies, flowers, and watering cans on sticker paper.

Using colored markers, write desired phrases on seed packet frames.

Trim photos to fit into stamped frames and cut out all stamped images to make stickers.

Lay-out the page and carefully adhere all photos and stamped image stickers into position on the background paper.

NEW YEAR'S EVE

Shown on page 50.

Using rubber stamps, stamp small balloons randomly over the entire surface of white glossy paper to create backgrounds.

Stamp several additional balloons and banner on sticker paper.

Using colored markers, write the desired phrase on the banner.

Trim photos as desired. Adhere photos on coordinating colors of paper and trim to a $^1/_4$" mat.

Cut out all stamped images to make stickers.

Lay-out the pages and carefully adhere all photos and stamped image stickers into position on the background paper.

BEAR & ME

Shown on page 50.

Using rubber stamps, stamp splatter designs randomly over the entire surface of white glossy paper to create backgrounds.

Stamp wood frames, pencils, paintbrushes, easel, bags, and banner on sticker paper.

Stamp or write the desired phrase on the banner and in the center of the easel.

Trim photos to fit into stamped frames and cut out all stamped images to make stickers. If desired, silhouette one photo.

Lay-out the pages and carefully adhere all photos and stamped image stickers into position on the background paper.

Jake and
Colby!
Jake and
Colby!
Just
Jake!

New Years Eve '96
CALEB
BEAR AND ME

White Pattern Backgrounds

To create a background that truly makes photos float, this technique should be used.

Choose a background paper that goes with the photos, then choose a rubber stamp that will make a pleasing image when repeated.

Color the rubber stamp with white pigment ink from an ink pad, but try not to get too much ink on the stamp or it will appear mushy.

Stamp the image several times keeping the images from touching. Create a varied, loose pattern across the entire page.

It is best to let the background paper dry overnight before beginning the page layout.

CHINA

Shown on page 51.

Using rubber stamps, randomly stamp gingko leaves and dragonflies with white over the entire surface of brown paper to create a background.

Stamp and emboss several gingko leaves and dragonflies with white on tan paper.

Stamp several more gingko leaves with black on tan paper.

Using deckled paper edgers, trim photos as desired. Double mat photos on black and white paper trimmed with deckled paper edgers.

Cut out all stamped images to make stickers.

Lay-out the page and carefully adhere all photos and stamped image stickers into position on the background paper.

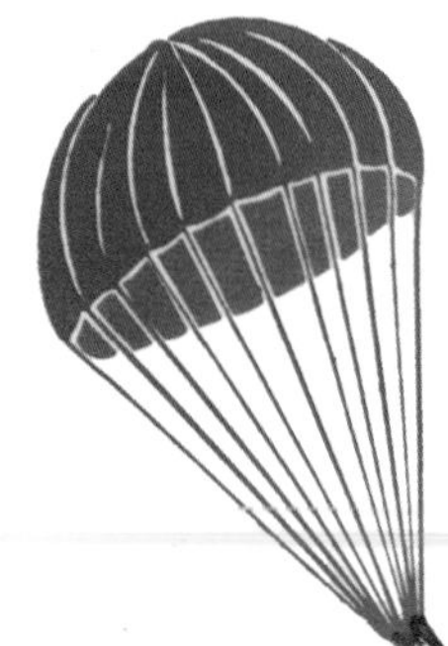

WARREN SKYDIVES

Shown on page 53.

Using rubber stamps, randomly stamp parachutes with white over the entire surface of brown paper to create a background.

Stamp three or four parachutes, newspaper frame, and helicopter on sticker paper.

Using a colored marker, write the desired headline on newspaper.

Trim one photo to fit into stamped frame and cut out all stamped images to make stickers. If desired, silhouette one or more photos.

Lay-out the page and carefully adhere all photos and stamped image stickers into position on the background paper.

FOURTH OF JULY

Shown on page 54.

Using rubber stamps, randomly stamp stars with white over the entire surface of one piece of red paper and one piece of blue paper to create a background.

Stamp firecrackers, flags, jars, calendar, and banner on sticker paper. Stamp "JULY" on the calendar.

Stamp or write the desired phrase on the banner.

Trim two photos to fit into stamped jars. Trim remaining photos as desired. Double mat photos on blue and white paper. Trim white paper with zigzag paper edgers.

Cut out all stamped images to make stickers.

Lay-out the pages and carefully adhere all photos and stamped image stickers into position on the background paper.

WE LOVE YOU SANTA

Shown on page 54.

Using rubber stamps, randomly stamp holly with white over the entire surface of one piece of green paper to create a background.

Stamp Christmas ornaments, ribbons, and scroll on sticker paper.

Stamp or write the desired phrase on the scroll.

Trim photos as desired. Double mat photos on white and red paper.

Cut out all stamped images to make stickers.

Lay-out the page and carefully adhere all photos and stamped image stickers into position on the background paper.

A SPECIAL DAY

Shown on page 54.

Using rubber stamps, randomly stamp small flowers with white over the entire surface of one piece of purple paper to create a background.

Stamp locket on sticker paper. Stamp and emboss small flowers with white on purple paper.

Using a colored marker, write the desired phrase in the center of the locket.

Trim photos as desired. Adhere photos on white paper and trim to a 1/4" mat. Trim one photo to fit inside the remaining side of locket.

Cut out all stamped images to make stickers.

Lay-out the page and carefully adhere all photos and stamped image stickers into position on the background paper.

DAILY TIMES 25¢
WARREN SKYDIVES!
E
P
C

JULY
COLBY
We Love You, SANTA
Maid of Honor my sister Kim

Stamped Newspaper Background

This basic background stamping method works in a variety of album page designs. The method is completed by coloring the newspaper design stamp with a brush art marker (typically black) and stamping the image in a varied repeating pattern until the page is full. Remember to stamp off the edge of the paper for a complete background image.

HAM BROTHERS

Shown on page 55.

Using rubber stamps, randomly stamp newspaper background with brown over the entire surface of white paper to create a background.

Stamp newspaper frame and photo corners on sticker paper.

Using a black marker, write the desired headline on newspaper frame and write additional phrases on various pieces of sticker paper.

Using deckled paper edgers, trim photos as desired.

Cut out all stamped images to make stickers.

Using a black marker, outline sticker paper with phrases.

Lay-out the page and carefully adhere all photos and stamped image stickers into position on the background paper.

LAS VEGAS!

Shown on page 57.

Using rubber stamps, randomly stamp and emboss newspaper background with white over the entire surface of black paper to create a background. Pull small pigment ink pads across the page to produce a rainbow color effect.

Stamp and emboss photo corners with white on bright colors of paper.

Stamp banner on sticker paper.

Using a colored marker, write the desired phrase on the banner.

Trim photos as desired. Adhere photos on coordinating colors of paper and trim to a 1/16" mat. Mount again on white paper and trim to a two-sided 1/4" drop shadow.

Cut out all stamped images to make stickers.

Lay-out the page and carefully adhere all photos and stamped image stickers into position on the background paper.

COACH OF THE YEAR

Shown on page 58.

Using rubber stamps, randomly stamp newspaper background with black over the entire surface of white paper to create a background.

Stamp camera frame, notebooks, megaphones, and pompom on sticker paper.

Cut strips of sticker paper and, using a black marker, outline each strip. Write the desired phrases on the strips.

Trim one photo to fit into camera frame and two photos to fit on top of notebooks. Trim remaining photos as desired. Adhere photos on black paper and trim to a 1/4" mat.

Cut out all stamped images to make stickers.

Lay-out the page and carefully adhere all photos and stamped image stickers into position on the background paper.

Using a gray marker, highlight two sides of photos.

DADDY'S HOME

Shown on page 5.

Using rubber stamps, randomly stamp newspaper background with black over the entire surface of white paper to create a background.

Stamp rope frames and newspaper frames on sticker paper.

Using a black marker, write the desired headlines on newspapers.

Trim photos to fit into stamped frames and cut out all stamped images to make stickers.

Lay-out the page and carefully adhere all photos and stamped image stickers into position on the background paper.

Using a gray marker, highlight two sides of photo frames.

Las Vegas!

COACH OF
THE YEAR
STATE
CHAMPS
LADY HAWKS
ASST. COACH
L.H.H.S.

Stamped Landscape Backgrounds

Par-fect Day

By using soft colored background papers, a wonderful landscape can be created with your favorite rubber stamps.

The possibilities are endless — from a background that gives a general feeling of the location where the photos were taken to creating an entire background scene in which photo silhouettes can be placed.

An important tip in selecting background paper is to choose something that is easy to stamp on — nothing with too much texture is recommended!

PAR-FECT DAY

Shown on page 59.

Using rubber stamps, randomly stamp grass in multiple shades of green across the foreground of white glossy paper. Layer grass to add depth and shadows.

Stamp clouds across top of page. Stamp extra clouds on scrap paper and cut out. Place cut out clouds over stamped clouds to "mask off."

Sponge in skyline with sky blue. Remove masking.

Stamp palm trees along the horizon.

Stamp photo corners, golf bags, golf balls, golf flags, banner, and additional palm trees on sticker paper.

Using a colored marker, write the desired phrase on the banner.

Trim photos as desired. Adhere photos on brown kraft paper and trim to a 1/4" mat.

Cut out all stamped images to make stickers.

Lay-out the page and carefully adhere all photos and stamped image stickers into position on the background paper.

SUMMER DAYS

Shown on page 61.

Using rubber stamps, randomly stamp grass in multiple shades of green across the foreground of white glossy paper. Layer grass to add depth and shadows.

Stamp a picket fence along the horizon. Stamp trees, flowers, and butterflies.

Stamp banner on sticker paper.

Using a colored marker, write the desired phrase on the banner.

Trim photos as desired. Adhere photos on gray paper and trim to a 1/8" mat. If desired, silhouette one photo.

Cut out all stamped images to make stickers.

Lay-out the page and carefully adhere all photos and stamped image stickers into position on the background paper.

Using a fine-tip marker, add butterfly trails made from very small dots.

VENEZUELA

Shown on page 62.

Using rubber stamps, randomly stamp tropical leaves in multiple shades of green in a border around the edges of off-white fiber paper. Layer leaves to add depth and shadows.

Stamp small wildflowers.

Lightly sponge over stamped area with light green to blend.

Stamp banner on brown kraft paper.

Stamp twig frames and several snakes on sticker paper.

Using a colored marker, write the desired phrase on the banner.

Trim two photos to fit into stamped frames. Using deckled paper edgers, trim remaining photos as desired. Adhere photos on brown kraft paper trimmed with deckled paper edgers. If desired, silhouette one photo.

Cut out all stamped images to make stickers.

Lay-out the page and carefully adhere all photos and stamped image stickers into position on the background paper.

Summer Days

VENEZUELA....
Crawling with Wildlife

White Embossed Frames

When working with stamped photo frames, there are many techniques that can be used for extra pizzazz. Embossing in white is very dramatic and the technique is fairly simple.

After choosing a frame, decide what color of background paper to use.

Apply embossing ink to the rubber stamp frame. Since most frames are larger in size, it is easier to lay the rubber stamp, rubber side up, on the work surface and place the embossing ink pad onto the stamp.

Stamp it on paper and immediately apply the embossing powder liberally. Pour the extra powder back into the container and tap the paper a few times to completely remove all the excess powder. If preferred, a small paintbrush can be used to remove stray powder.

Heat the image with an embossing heat gun, taking care not to hold the paper too close to the heat source as this can cause the paper to curl. Once cool, cut the frame out.

WINTER FUN

Shown on page 63.

Using rubber stamps, stamp and emboss snowflakes with white over the entire surface of blue paper to create a background.

Stamp and emboss wood frames, camera frame, and banner with white on black paper.

Stamp film roll frame and snow (made with sand stamp) on sticker paper.

Using a white opaque correction pen, write the desired phrase on the banner.

Trim photos to fit into stamped frames and cut out all stamped images to make stickers.

Lay-out the page and carefully adhere all photos and stamped image stickers into position on the background paper.

UNDERWATER ADVENTURE

Shown on page 65.

Using rubber stamps, stamp and emboss rope frames with white on blue paper.

Stamp sand, seashells, sand castle, tropical fish, and banner on sticker paper.

Stamp or write the desired phrase on the banner.

Trim photos to fit into stamped frames and cut out all stamped images to make stickers. If desired, silhouette one photo.

Lay-out the page and carefully adhere all photos and stamped image stickers into position on the background paper.

LUNCH ON THE BEACH

Shown on page 66.

Using rubber stamps, stamp and emboss clouds, sun, and sand with white on gray paper to create backgrounds.

Stamp and emboss wood frames, seashells, geese, sand, and banner with white on black paper.

Using a white opaque correction pen, write the desired phrase on the banner.

Trim photos to fit into stamped frames and cut out all stamped images to make stickers. If desired, silhouette one or more photos.

Lay-out the pages and carefully adhere all photos and stamped image stickers into position on the background paper.

AIR SHOW

Shown on page 66.

Using rubber stamps, stamp and emboss stars with white on navy blue paper to create backgrounds.

Stamp and emboss rope frames with white on a variety of bright colored paper.

Stamp flags and airplane cloud frame on sticker paper.

Stamp or write the desired phrase in the center of the airplane cloud frame.

Trim photos to fit into stamped frames and cut out all stamped images to make stickers.

If desired, invitations and ticket stubs can be used in the layout to add interest and provide journaling information. If they are too large to be used, they can be reduced in color or in black and white on any photocopier.

Lay-out the pages and carefully adhere all photos and stamped image stickers into position on the background paper.

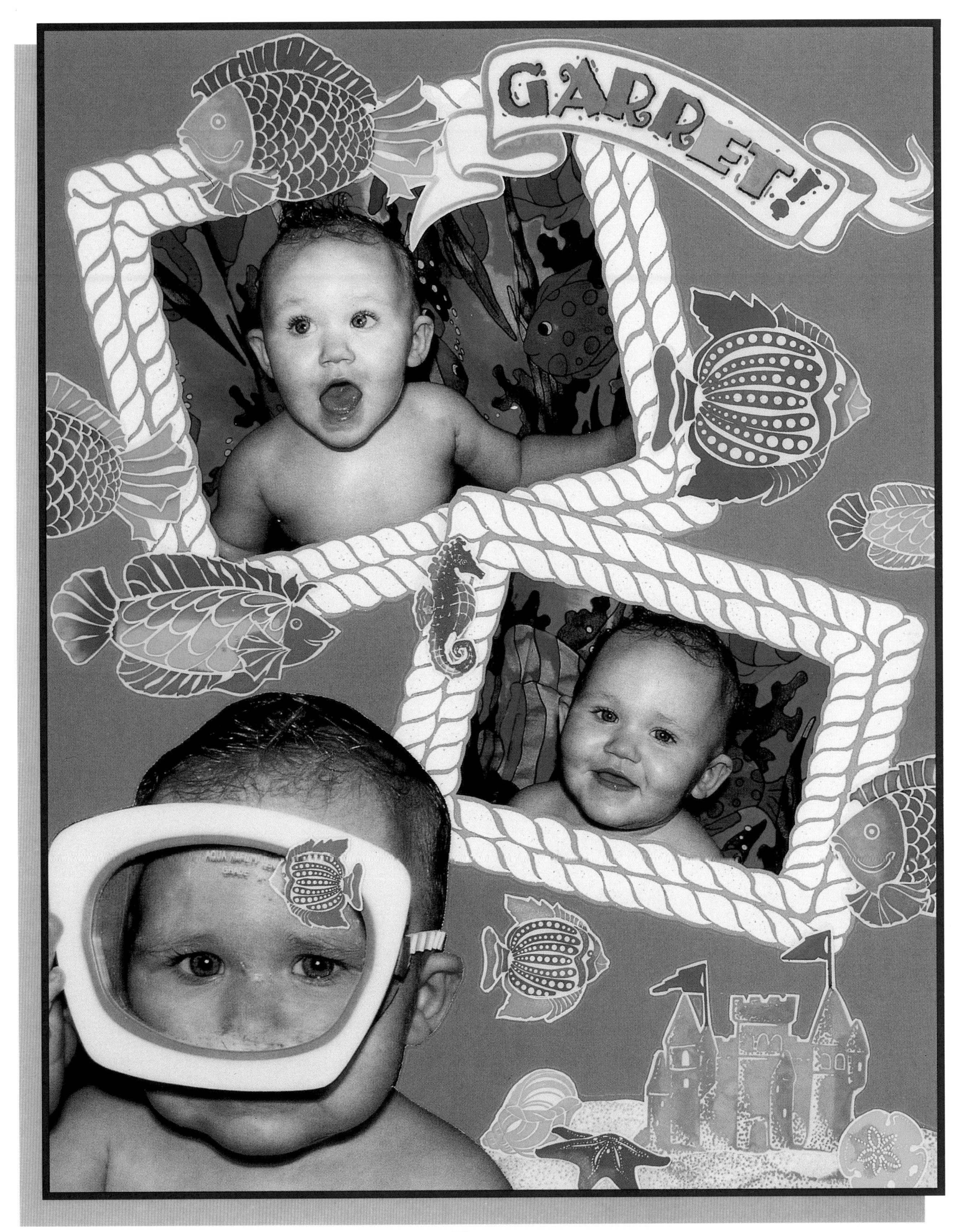
GARRET!

Lunch on the Beach

AIR SHOW
Commanding Generals'
VIP SEAT
FRIDAY APRIL 25, 1997
Gates open: 7am
Located on flightline at far left of grandstands
Please look for VIP entrance and
present this ticket for seating.

The Commanding Generals
Marine Corps Air Station El Toro and Third Marine Aircraft Wing
cordially invite you to attend
a Garden Party
on Friday, the twenty-fifth of April
at half past four o'clock
at Quarters B, MCAS El Toro
Please present this card at the entrance to the Quarters
Military: Uniform of the Day
Civilian: Casual Attire
This invitation is not transferable

Metallic Embossed Frames

If glitz and glamour are what is desired, then check out this sparkling technique!

After choosing a frame, decide what color of background paper to use. For a truly dramatic look, try embossing on black paper.

Choosing an embossing powder color will be difficult — there are at least 100 different tones and tinsellette powders available.

Apply embossing ink to the rubber stamp frame. Since most frames are larger in size, it is easier to lay the rubber stamp, rubber side up, on the work surface and place the embossing ink pad onto the stamp.

Stamp it on paper and immediately apply the embossing powder liberally. Pour the extra powder back into the container and tap the paper a few times to completely remove all the excess powder. If preferred, a small paintbrush can be used to remove stray powder.

Heat the image with an embossing heat gun, taking care not to hold the paper too close to the heat source as this can cause the paper to curl. Once cool, cut the frame out.

ELEPHANTS

Shown on page 67.

Using rubber stamps, stamp and emboss bamboo with a natural blend of metallic powders vertically over brown kraft paper to create a background.

Stamp and emboss bamboo frames with pewter embossing over gold and silver ink on brown kraft paper. Stamp and emboss banner with gold on black paper.

Using a metallic gold pen, write the desired phrase on the banner.

Trim photos to fit into stamped frames and cut out all stamped images to make stickers.

Lay-out the page and carefully adhere all photos and stamped image stickers into position on the background paper.

COLORFUL SRI LANKA

Shown on page 69.

Using rubber stamps, stamp and emboss photo corners, tasseled cording frames, and banners with gold on black paper.

Using a metallic gold pen, write the desired phrases on the banners.

Trim one photo to fit into stamped frame. Trim two photos as desired. Adhere photos on gold paper and trim to a 1/4" mat.

Cut tassels off two frames to make two photo corners and cut out all stamped images to make stickers.

Lay-out the page and carefully adhere all photos and stamped image stickers into position on the background paper.

Using a metallic gold pen, enhance page by drawing a line connecting photo corners.

BANGKOK

Shown on page 70.

Using rubber stamps, stamp and emboss bamboo frames, one ornate frame, and several clusters of camellias with gold on black paper.

Stamp and emboss several leaves with metallic green on black paper.

Stamp and emboss butterflies and additional clusters of camellias and leaves with metallic red, metallic green, and metallic blue on brown kraft paper.

Trim photos to fit into stamped frames and cut out all stamped images to make stickers. If desired, silhouette one or more photos.

Lay-out the pages and carefully adhere all photos and stamped image stickers into position on the background paper.

BIRTHDAY KING

Shown on page 70.

Using rubber stamps, stamp and emboss rope frames, one birthday cake frame, and several crowns with gold on black paper.

Stamp several balloons and ribbons on sticker paper.

Enhance candles and crowns with glitter.

Using a metallic gold pen, write the desired phrase in the center of the birthday cake frame.

Trim photos to fit into stamped frames and cut out all stamped images to make stickers. If desired, silhouette one photo.

Lay-out the pages and carefully adhere all photos and stamped image stickers into position on the background paper.

Enhance page by randomly adding small dots of silver glitter.

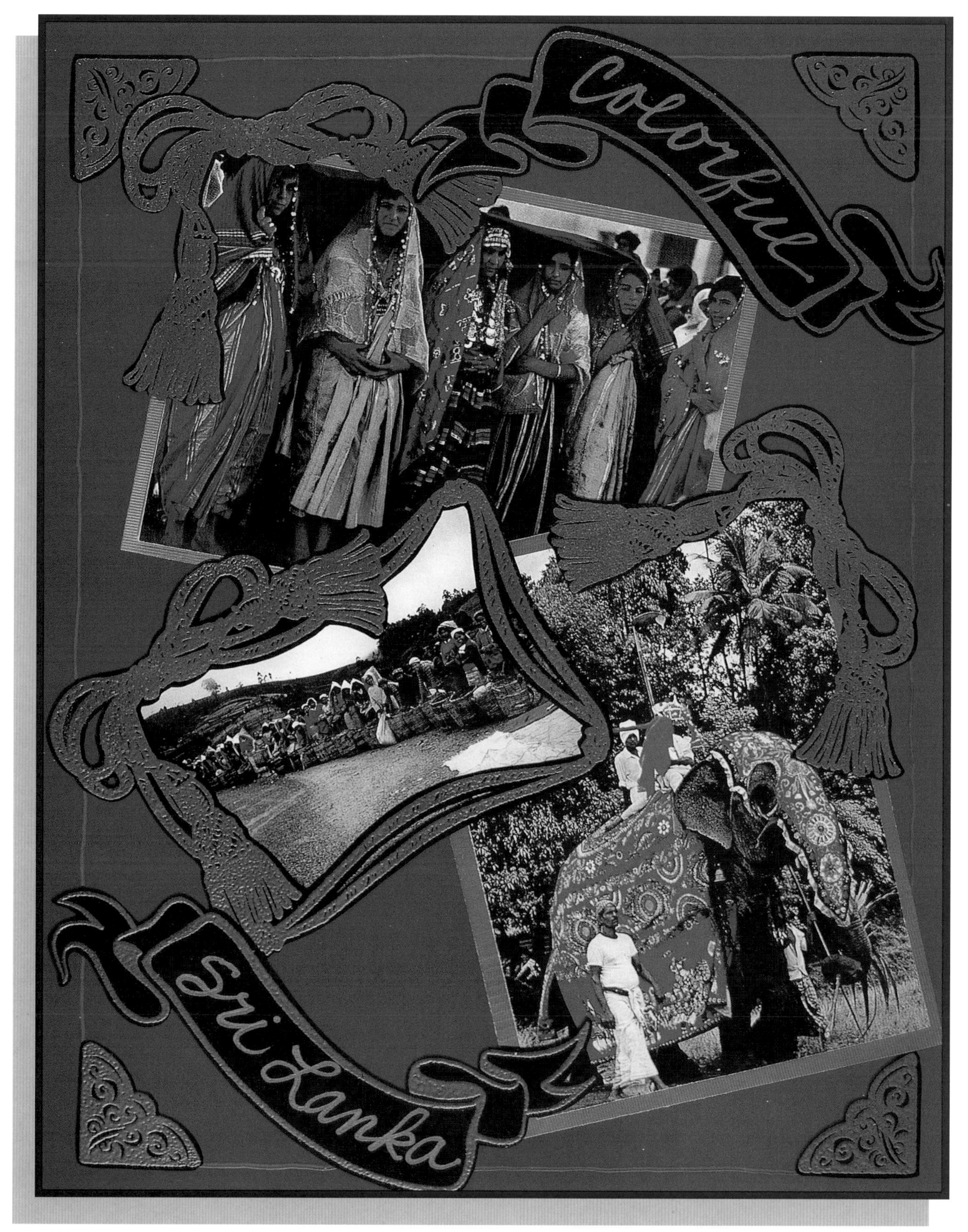
Colorful
Sri Lanka

Celebration
fit for
a King!!!

Brayered Pen Designs

Fun design backgrounds can be created by using brush art markers to draw images on a soft rubber brayer. Zigzags, X's and O's, confetti and stripes can be drawn.

Using the very tip of the marker, cover the entire surface of the rubber brayer with marks of various colors in chosen shapes. Work with the brayer resting on its handle. Turn roller with one hand and mark it as you turn.

For stripes, hold marker steady, brush tip touching roller, and turn roller with other hand, continuing stripe until it meets at the beginning. Repeat for each stripe. Roll over paper starting and stopping off the edges of the paper.

Remoisten roller by exhaling over the entire surface. Remoisten or re-ink as necessary to cover the entire page. Use firm, even pressure on white glossy paper.

HUGS & KISSES

Shown on page 71.

Draw X's and O's on a rubber brayer with different colors of markers and roll brayer over white paper to create a background.

Using rubber stamps, stamp stage frames, heart frames, and various sized hearts on sticker paper.

Trim photos to fit into stamped frames and cut out all stamped images to make stickers.

Lay-out the page and carefully adhere all photos and stamped image stickers into position on the background paper.

ZION NATIONAL PARK

Shown on page 73.

Draw "quotation marks" on a rubber brayer with shades of green and brown markers and roll brayer over white paper to create a background.

Using rubber stamps, stamp pine trees, mountains, rocky terrain, jeep, and directional sign on sticker paper.

Using a colored marker, write the desired phrase on the directional sign.

Trim photos as desired. Adhere photos on green and brown paper trimmed with deckled paper edgers.

Cut out all stamped images to make stickers.

Lay-out the page and carefully adhere all photos and stamped image stickers into position on the background paper.

PIRATE PARTY

Shown on page 74.

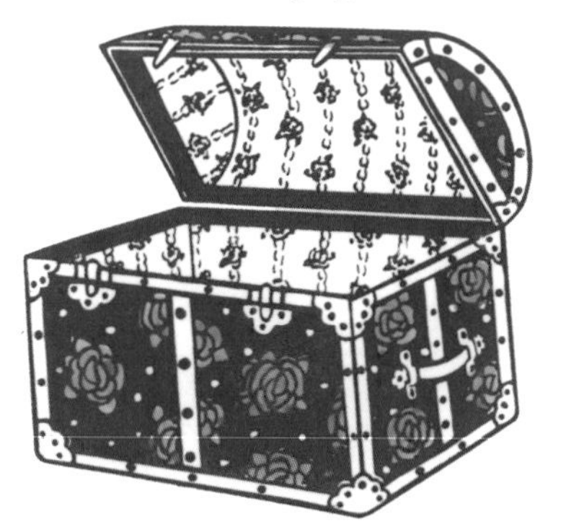

Draw confetti on a rubber brayer with the tips of different colors of markers and roll brayer over white paper to create backgrounds.

Using rubber stamps, stamp rope frames, small and large palm trees, treasure chest, small house, sand, and blank page on sticker paper.

Sand can be softened and blended by applying markers to a good quality make-up sponge.

Using colored markers, write on blank page to resemble a map. Embellish with drawings and tiny stamps.

Trim photos to fit into stamped frames and cut out all stamped images to make stickers. If desired, silhouette one or more photos.

Lay-out the pages and carefully adhere all photos and stamped image stickers into position on the background paper.

Small palm trees and small house can be placed appropriately on the map.

FEEDING THE HORSES

Shown on page 74.

Draw arrowhead stripes on a rubber brayer with different colors of markers and roll brayer over white paper to create a background.

Using rubber stamps, stamp fence, cacti, bandanas, sand, skull, and lasso on sticker paper.

Using a colored marker, write desired phrase in the center of the lasso.

Trim photos as desired. Adhere photos on brown paper and trim to a 1/4" mat.

Cut out all stamped images to make stickers.

Lay-out the page and carefully adhere all photos and stamped image stickers into position on the background paper.

LITTLE INDIANS

Shown on page 74.

Draw zigzags on a rubber brayer with different colors of markers and roll brayer over white paper to create a background.

Using rubber stamps, stamp southwest frames, pottery, cacti, and sun on sticker paper.

Trim photos to fit into stamped frames and cut out all stamped images to make stickers.

Lay-out the page and carefully adhere all photos and stamped image stickers into position on the background paper.

ZION
NATIONAL PARK
USA

PARTY
HERE!
CAPT. JAKE

Feeding the Horses

Brayered Plaid and Ginghams

This technique has many variations and takes a little practice.

A soft rubber brayer must be used. A 6" brayer is easier to control and covers more of the page at one time.

Lay the brayer, roller side up, toward you on a padded surface. Draw lines onto the brayer roller. This is done by drawing with one hand and turning the roller carefully with the other hand. Make all of the lines the same size and color or vary them.

Once all the lines have been drawn, roll the brayer across the chosen background paper, remembering to begin and end off the paper.

Exhale on the roller to re-moisten. Re-ink as necessary. Then turn the page the opposite direction. When finished, you will have a vibrant plaid or gingham design.

GRAMPA'S GIRL!

Happy Birthday

GRAMPA'S GIRL

Shown on page 75.

Draw lines in a variety of widths on a rubber brayer with different colors of markers and roll brayer diagonally over white paper to create a background.

Using rubber stamps, stamp birthday cake frames, balloons, ribbons, tag, and banner on sticker paper.

Using a colored marker, write the desired phrase on the banner. Stamp or write "HAPPY BIRTHDAY" in the center of the tag.

Trim photos to fit into stamped frames and cut out all stamped images to make stickers. If desired, silhouette one photo and mat.

Lay-out the page and carefully adhere all photos and stamped image stickers into position on the background paper.

MONTANA

Shown on page 77.

Draw lines in a variety of widths on a rubber brayer with different colors of markers and roll brayer vertically and horizontally over white paper to create a background.

Using rubber stamps, stamp twig frames, pine trees rocks, clouds, tent, and directional sign on sticker paper.

Using a colored marker, write the desired phrase on the directional sign.

Trim photos to fit into stamped frames and cut out all stamped images to make stickers.

Lay-out the page and carefully adhere all photos and stamped image stickers into position on the background paper.

BACKYARD SUMMER DAYS

Shown on page 78.

Draw wide lines on a rubber brayer with a yellow marker and roll brayer vertically and horizontally over white paper to create a background.

Using rubber stamps, stamp ribbon frames, heart frame, wildflower corners, and butterflies on sticker paper.

Using colored markers, write the desired phrase in the center of the heart frame.

Trim photos to fit into stamped frames and cut out all stamped images to make stickers. If desired, silhouette one photo.

Lay-out the page and carefully adhere all photos and stamped image stickers into position on the background paper.

LADYBUGS & IVY

Shown on page 79.

Draw wide lines on a rubber brayer with red markers and roll brayer diagonally in both directions over white paper to create a background.

Using rubber stamps, stamp and emboss twig frames with white on black paper.

Stamp a picket fence with climbing vines and flowers, ivy, and ladybugs on sticker paper.

Trim photos to fit into stamped frames and cut out all stamped images to make stickers. If desired, silhouette one photo.

Lay-out the page and carefully adhere all photos and stamped image stickers into position on the background paper.

WANTED

Shown on page 80.

Draw wide lines on a rubber brayer with a red marker and roll brayer vertically and horizontally over white paper to create a background.

Using rubber stamps, stamp wood frames, stars, cowboy hats, wanted poster, and banner on sticker paper.

Stamp or write the desired phrases on the wanted poster and the banner.

Trim photos to fit into stamped frames and cut out all stamped images to make stickers.

Lay-out the page and carefully adhere all photos and stamped image stickers into position on the background paper.

MONTANA!

Backyard
Summer Days!

WANTED
DEAD OR ALIVE
MICHAEL, the kid!
MICHAEL

Enhanced Brayered Backgrounds

Daddy's Day!

An enhanced version of the brayered plaids and ginghams, this technique also has many variations and takes a little practice. A soft rubber brayer must be used. A 6" brayer is easier to control and covers more of the page at one time.

Lay the brayer, roller side up, toward you on a padded surface. Draw lines onto the brayer roller. This is done by drawing with one hand and turning the roller carefully with the other hand. Make all of the lines the same size and color or vary them.

Once all the lines have been drawn, roll the brayer across the chosen background paper, remembering to begin and end off the paper.

Exhale on the roller to remoisten. Re-ink as necessary. Then turn the page the opposite direction. When finished, you will have a vibrant plaid or gingham design.

Using a fine tip black marker, draw lines on both sides of the brayered plaid. When finished, the plaid designs will have an added dimension.

DADDY'S DAY

Shown on page 81.

Draw lines in a variety of widths on a rubber brayer with blue and green markers and roll brayer vertically and horizontally over white paper to create a background. When dry, enhance plaid design with a fine-point black marker.

Using rubber stamps, stamp leaves and banner on sticker paper.

Using a colored marker, write the desired phrase on the banner.

Trim photos as desired. Adhere photos on navy blue paper and trim to a 1/4" mat.

Cut out all stamped images to make stickers.

Lay-out the page and carefully adhere all photos and stamped image stickers into position on the background paper.

RILEY

Shown on page 83.

Draw lines in two widths on a rubber brayer with different colors of markers and roll brayer vertically and horizontally over white paper to create a background. When dry, enhance plaid design with a fine-point black marker.

Using rubber stamps, stamp raffia frames, award ribbon, and banner on sticker paper.

Using a black marker, write the desired phrase in the center of the award ribbon.

Stamp or write the desired phrase on the banner.

Trim photos to fit into stamped frames and cut out all stamped images to make stickers. If desired, silhouette one photo.

Lay-out the page and carefully adhere all photos and stamped image stickers into position on the background paper.

BANDANAS

Shown on page 84.

Draw lines in two widths on a rubber brayer with red and blue markers and roll brayer diagonally in both directions over white paper to create a background. When dry, enhance plaid design with a fine-point black marker.

Using rubber stamps, stamp bandanas and banner on sticker paper.

Stamp or write the desired phrase on the banner.

Trim photos as desired. Double mat photos on white paper trimmed to a 1/8" mat followed by red paper on one photo, bright blue paper on one photo, and navy blue paper on one photo trimmed to a 1/4" mat.

Cut out all stamped images to make stickers.

Lay-out the page and carefully adhere all photos and stamped image stickers into position on the background paper.

1ST PLACE COUNTY FAIR
RILEY

BANDANAS

Brayered Image Backgrounds

Strawberries

Brayered backgrounds are done with a soft rubber brayer.

Color a rubber stamp with brush art markers and place it, colored side up, on a flat padded surface. Carefully roll the brayer across the stamp one or more times in different angles or positions on the rubber.

To create the background, roll the brayer across the background paper, starting and ending off the paper for a finished look.

White glossy paper is the recommended choice of paper.

Re-ink and repeat as desired.

FRESH STRAWBERRIES

Shown on page 85.

Color a strawberry rubber stamp and roll a rubber brayer across the stamp one or more times. Roll the brayer over white paper to create a background. Enhance the background by stamping additional strawberries on the white paper.

Using rubber stamps, stamp jars, wood crate, fabric, boardwalk, banner, and more strawberries on sticker paper.

Using a colored marker, write the desired phrase on the banner.

Using colonial paper edgers, trim photos as desired. Adhere one photo on red paper and one photo on green paper and trim to a 1/4" mat. If desired, silhouette one photo.

Cut out all stamped images to make stickers.

Lay-out the page and carefully adhere all photos and stamped image stickers into position on the background paper.

PUMPKIN PATCH

Shown on page 87.

Color an autumn leaf rubber stamp in shades of gold, red, burgundy, green, orange, and brown and roll a rubber brayer across the stamp one or more times. Roll the brayer over white paper to create a background. Enhance the background by stamping additional autumn leaves on the white paper.

Using rubber stamps, stamp wood frames, camera frame, banner, and more leaves on sticker paper.

Using a colored marker, write the desired phrase on the banner.

Trim photos to fit into stamped frames and cut out all stamped images to make stickers.

Lay-out the page and carefully adhere all photos and stamped image stickers into position on the background paper.

JUICY, JUICY, JUICY

Shown on page 88.

Color a watermelon slice rubber stamp and roll a rubber brayer across the stamp one or more times. Roll the brayer over white paper to create a background. Enhance the background by stamping additional slices of watermelon on the white paper.

Using rubber stamps, stamp banner and more slices of watermelon on sticker paper.

Stamp or write the desired phrase on the banner.

Trim photos as desired. Adhere photos on black paper and trim to a 1/4" mat. If desired, silhouette one photo.

Cut out all stamped images to make stickers. Cut slices of watermelons in half to make photo corners.

Lay-out the page and carefully adhere all photos and stamped image stickers into position on the background paper.

Pumpkin Patch

Caleb

Brayered Landscapes

Alaska

When lovely landscape backgrounds are desired, but you cannot imagine stamping several separate images to create album pages, then brayered landscapes are perfect.

A soft rubber brayer is needed and your choice of rubber stamps.

Color a rubber stamp with brush art markers and place it, colored side up, on a flat padded surface. Carefully roll the brayer across the stamp one or more times in different angles or positions on the rubber.

To create the background, roll the brayer across the background paper, starting and ending off the paper for a finished look.

Re-ink and repeat as desired.

To complete the landscape, stamp some images directly onto the background paper. This will give dimension to the background because of the textures of stamped images and the brayered images which will be in reverse.

ALASKA

Shown on page 89.

Brayer bare trees, water, clouds, and rocks over white paper to create a background. Enhance the background by stamping additional images on the white paper and sponging.

Using rubber stamps, stamp photo corners, additional bare trees, and banner on sticker paper.

Using a colored marker, write the desired phrase on the banner.

Trim photos as desired. Adhere photos on brown kraft paper and trim to a 1/4" mat. If desired, silhouette one photo.

Cut out all stamped images to make stickers.

Lay-out the page and carefully adhere all photos and stamped image stickers into position on the background paper.

BOUNTIFUL HARVEST

Shown on page 91.

Brayer pumpkins and haystacks over white paper to create a background. Enhance the background by stamping additional images on the white paper. Stamp grass, spiders, webs, and a sun directly onto the page.

Using rubber stamps, stamp wood frames, frogs, pumpkins, and haystacks on sticker paper.

Using a colored marker, write the desired phrase on one of the pumpkins.

Trim photos to fit into stamped frames and cut out all stamped images to make stickers. If desired, silhouette one photo.

Lay-out the page and carefully adhere all photos and stamped image stickers into position on the background paper.

BE ALL THAT YOU CAN BE!

Shown on page 92.

Brayer tall pine trees and grass across the top of white paper to create a background. Enhance the background by stamping additional images on the white paper. Stamp rocks and clouds directly onto the page.

Using rubber stamps, stamp tents, jeep, and banner on sticker paper.

Using a colored marker, write the desired phrase on the banner.

Trim photos as desired. If desired, silhouette one or more photos.

Cut out all stamped images to make stickers.

Lay-out the page and carefully adhere all photos and stamped image stickers into position on the background paper.

PUMPKIN
PATCH!

BE ALL that you can BE.....
HOOAH!
USA

Brayered Rainbow Pad with Shadows and Highlights

To begin this background, choose a rainbow pad that will add to your entire page design.

Using a black foam brayer, roll it several times across the ink pad until the entire roller is covered with ink. Then roll it across your glossy paper, remembering to begin and end off the paper, until the entire page is covered.

Roll the brayer back and forth over the same area until desired intensity of color is achieved. The brayer will need to be re-inked to keep the color consistent.

This technique can be done horizontally, vertically, or diagonally.

BEACH PARTY

Shown on page 93.

Using a floral rainbow pad, brayer the background horizontally.

Using rubber stamps, stamp rope frames, beach balls, seashells, sand, sandcastle, and birthday cake frame on sticker paper.

Using colored markers, write the desired phrase in the center of the birthday cake frame.

Trim photos to fit into stamped frames and cut out all stamped images to make stickers. If desired, silhouette one photo.

Lay-out the page and carefully adhere all photos and stamped image stickers into position on the background paper.

Stamp butterflies directly onto the page. Using a fine-tip marker, add butterfly trails made from very small dots.

EASTER MORNING

Shown on page 95.

Using a rainbow pad of pink, purple, blue, and green, brayer the background horizontally.

Using rubber stamps, stamp ribbons, butterflies, grass, sun, bunny, and window on sticker paper. Lightly sponge over grass to blend colors.

Trim photos as desired and cut out all stamped images to make stickers. Trim top edge of grass with ripple paper edgers. If desired, silhouette one photo.

Lay-out the page and carefully adhere all photos and stamped image stickers into position on the background paper.

Using a white opaque pen, add butterfly trails made from very small dots.

Enhance the grass with small flower stickers.

DODGERS BASEBALL

Shown on page 96.

Using a rainbow pad of blues and greens, brayer the background horizontally.

Using rubber stamps, stamp and emboss wood frame with white on black paper.

Stamp camera frame, billboard frame, grass, bats, and baseballs on sticker paper. Lightly sponge over grass to blend colors.

Trim photos to fit into stamped frames and cut out all stamped images to make stickers. Trim top edge of grass with ripple paper edgers. If desired, silhouette one photo.

Lay-out the page and carefully adhere all photos and stamped image stickers into position on the background paper.

Using a white opaque pen, add dashed lines to give the illusion of motion.

Enhance the page with a ticket stub from an actual event to serve as the journaling information.

HAM
GAME PRICE LEVEL
3 19.00 Dug
ADMIT ONE
Jackie Robinson - broke Baseball's color barrier and was named the league's first Rookie of the Year in 1947, an award later named after him.
SUBJECT TO THE CONDITIONS SET FORTH ON THE BACK HEREOF.
5 DD 3
AISLE ROW SEAT
Thu Apr 03, 1997
7:05 PM
Season Ticket
Dodgers
vs
PHILLIES
40th Season
PIAZZA
KARROS
23

To begin this background, choose a rainbow pad that will add to your entire page design. Using a black foam brayer, roll it several times across the ink pad until the entire roller is covered with ink. Then roll it across your glossy paper, remembering to begin and end off the paper, until the entire page is covered.

Roll the brayer back and forth over the same area until desired intensity of color is achieved. The brayer will need to be re-inked to keep the color consistent.

Once the entire page is covered with the rainbow pad ink, choose brush art markers that are similar shades or tones to your rainbow pad. Add "shadow" designs, such as zigzags, wavy lines, scallops, or dots. To add the "highlights," select an opaque white correction pen with a ballpoint tip. Draw directly along some of your "shadows" as well as adding some additional "highlights."

PLAY BALL

Shown on page 97.

Using a bright colored rainbow pad, brayer the background horizontally. Using coordinating markers, shadow across page in a wave-like pattern. Using a white opaque pen, add highlighting.

Using rubber stamps, stamp photo corners, sun, and banner on sticker paper.

Using a colored marker, write the desired phrase on the banner.

Trim photos as desired. Adhere photos on bright blue paper and trim to a 1/4" mat.

Cut out all stamped images to make stickers.

Lay-out the page and carefully adhere all photos and stamped image stickers into position on the background paper.

Stamp butterflies directly onto the page. Using a fine-tip marker, add butterfly trails made from very small dots.

SWEET AS A ROSE

Shown on page 99.

Using a pastel rainbow pad, brayer the background horizontally. Using coordinating markers, shadow across page in a soft wave-like pattern. Using a white opaque pen, add highlighting.

Using rubber stamps, stamp rope frames, clusters of roses, and heart on sticker paper.

Using a colored marker, write the desired phrase in the center of the heart.

Trim photos to fit into stamped frames and cut out all stamped images to make stickers.

Lay-out the page and carefully adhere all photos and stamped image stickers into position on the background paper.

INDIANS

Shown on page 100.

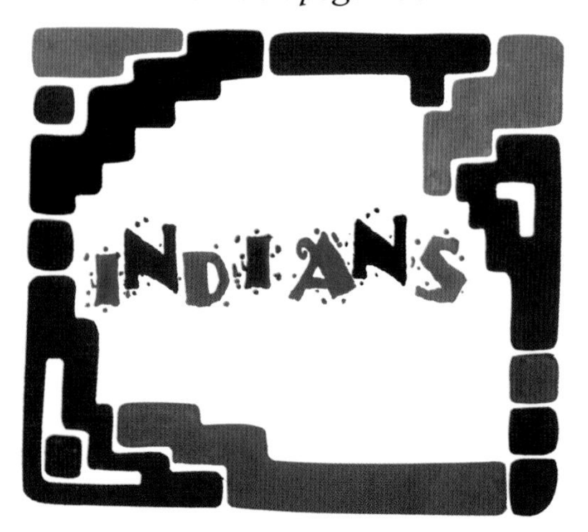

Using an earth tone rainbow pad, brayer the background vertically. Using coordinating markers, shadow down page in a variety of horizontal patterns. Using a white opaque pen, add highlighting.

Using rubber stamps, stamp adobe frames and banner on sticker paper.

Using a colored marker, write the desired phrase on the banner.

Trim photos to fit into stamped frames and cut out all stamped images to make stickers. If desired, silhouette one photo.

Lay-out the page and carefully adhere all photos and stamped image stickers into position on the background paper.

Sweet as a Rose!

INDIANS!

Brayered Rainbow Pad Resist Backgrounds

Hawaii

These dramatic backgrounds are created in three steps. First, using a black foam brayer and your choice of rainbow stamp pad, roll the brayer across the ink pad several times until the entire brayer roller is covered with ink.

Using glossy paper, begin rolling the brayer across the paper, beginning and ending off the paper. Roll it across the paper several times in a consistent motion, until the entire background paper is covered. Re-ink the brayer to maintain the color intensity. Allow ink to dry.

Second, apply rubber cement in a free form design — do not try to make perfect shapes. Allow rubber cement to dry thoroughly.

Third, with the rubber cement still on the paper, apply a layer of black ink using a soft rubber brayer covered with black brush art marker.

Once the entire page is rich and dark with the black ink, allow it to dry overnight. Then, using a rubber cement pick-up, remove all of the rubber cement and you will see this dramatic background appear.

TROPICAL PARADISE

Shown on page 101.

Using a tropical rainbow pad and a black inked brayer, create a brayered resist background.

Using rubber stamps, stamp colored flowers and banner on sticker paper.

Using colored markers, write the desired phrase on the banner.

Using wave paper edgers, trim photos as desired. Adhere photos on black paper and trim to a 1/4" mat.

Cut out all stamped images to make stickers.

Lay-out the page and carefully adhere all photos and stamped image stickers into position on the background paper.

HIP HIP HOORAY

Shown on page 103.

Using a rainbow pad of blues and greens and a black inked brayer, create a brayered resist background.

Using rubber stamps, stamp firecrackers, birthday cake, and banner on sticker paper.

Using a colored marker, write the desired phrase on the banner.

Draw a number on sticker paper to correspond with the appropriate age and cut out.

Trim photos as desired. Adhere photos on coordinating paper and trim to a 1/8" mat.

Cut out all stamped images to make stickers.

Lay-out the page and carefully adhere all photos and stamped image stickers into position on the background paper.

BRIDGE CROSSING

Shown on page 104.

Using an earthtone rainbow pad and a black inked brayer, create a brayered resist background.

Using rubber stamps, stamp frogs, directional sign, and twisting leaves on sticker paper.

Using a colored marker, write the desired phrase on the directional sign.

Trim photos as desired. Double mat photos on orange and tan paper.

Cut out all stamped images to make stickers.

Lay-out the page and carefully adhere all photos and stamped image stickers into position on the background paper.

Hip, Hip, Hooray
8

BRIDGE
CROSSING

Sponge Brayer Watercolor Backgrounds

Dual Watercolor Landscapes: These backgrounds must be done on two sheets of paper side-by-side. To create a continuous scene, they must be watercolored and stamped together.

Glossy or matte finish paper can be used, but the additional stamping will be brighter when done on glossy paper.

Dual watercolor is done with a soft sponge brayer. Apply color in random stripes and marks using brush art markers. Then, lightly mist the whole roller with water. The upper part of the page will be the sky, so start with shades of blue, adding some pink, lavender, or yellow for sunrise or sunset tones. Roll the brayer over the top one-third or one-half of the page. The sponge then needs to be washed and squeezed, but not dried. Keeping the brayer damp allows you to skip the "misting" step for the next applications.

For the lower landscape, apply earthtones to the brayer and roll over the bottom area of the page slightly overlapping the sky.

If a water background is desired, as in the beach scenes, allow for a third section at the bottom and use appropriate colors.

Allow pages to dry thoroughly before adding any additional stamping.

Rubber Brayer Landscapes: Brayered images are the softer reverse background images. Use a soft rubber brayer, between 4"- and 6"-wide.

Ink a rubber stamp and place it, inked side up, on a flat surface. Carefully roll the brayer over the stamp using moderate pressure.

Roll the brayer over the page, starting with an uninked portion of the roller. This prevents a partial image. Roll all the way off the other side of the page. Before re-inking the stamp, exhale on it and stamp directly onto the page. Re-ink and stamp some brighter images as desired.

SPRING HAS SPRUNG

Shown on page 105.

Using the dual watercolor technique in blue for the sky and green and yellow green for the grass, create a landscape background.

Brayer the mountains onto the page and stamp additional mountains.

Using rubber stamps, stamp clouds, sun, butterflies, grassy meadow, and wild grass directly onto the page.

Stamp wood frame, hot air balloons, field flowers, and directional sign on sticker paper.

Stamp or write the desired phrase on the directional sign.

Trim photo to fit inside stamped frame and cut out all stamped images to make stickers. If desired, silhouette one photo.

Lay-out the page and carefully adhere all photos and stamped image stickers into position on the background paper.

HOME ON THE RANGE

Shown on page 107.

Using the dual watercolor technique in blue with accents of yellow and fuschia for the sky and beige, mauve, and gold for the earth, create a landscape background.

Brayer the buttes onto the page and stamp additional buttes.

Using rubber stamps, stamp clouds, sun, old tree, sand, and grassy meadow directly onto the page.

Stamp twig frames, foxglove, and banner on sticker paper.

Using a colored marker, write the desired phrase on the banner.

Trim photos to fit inside stamped frames and cut out all stamped images to make stickers. If desired, silhouette one or more photos.

Lay-out the page and carefully adhere all photos and stamped image stickers into position on the background paper.

COSTA RICA

Shown on page 108.

Using the dual watercolor technique with just a small amount of blue sky, green and yellow in the center area, and yellow and gold for the sandy bottom, create a landscape background.

Brayer the bamboo onto the pages and stamp additional bamboo stalks.

Using rubber stamps, stamp palm fronds, jungle leaves, ferns, and other leaf patterns directly onto the pages.

Stamp bamboo frames, several orchids, and banner on sticker paper.

Using colored markers, write the desired phrase on the banner.

Trim photos to fit inside stamped frames and cut out all stamped images to make stickers.

Lay-out the pages and carefully adhere all photos and stamped image stickers into position on the background paper.

BEACH BUDDIES

Shown on page 108.

Using the dual watercolor technique in blue, lavender, and turquoise for the sky, yellow and gold for the sand, and blue and turquoise for the water, create a landscape background.

Brayer and stamp the palm trees onto the pages.

Using rubber stamps, stamp clouds, sand, waves, grassy meadow, and rocks directly onto the pages.

Stamp palm trees, sandcastle, plane with cloud, and sun on sticker paper.

Using a colored marker, write the desired phrase in the center of the airplane cloud.

Trim photos as desired. Double mat photos on yellow and blue paper. Trim blue paper with wave paper edgers. If desired, silhouette one or more photos.

Cut out all stamped images to make stickers.

Lay-out the pages and carefully adhere all photos and stamped image stickers into position on the background paper.

at Home on the
"Rankin Range"

Costa Rica!

BEACH BUDDIES

Brayered Reverse with Spatters

This combination background method adds depth to any album page design. A soft rubber brayer and one or more rubber stamps is needed.

Color the stamp with brush art markers and place it, color side up, on a flat padded surface. Carefully roll the brayer across the stamp one or more times in different angles or positions on the rubber roller.

Roll the brayer across the background paper, starting and ending off the paper. Re-ink and repeat as desired.

Stamp some images directly on the paper for more intense color and opposite direction images. Then, using a paint splatter design rubber stamp and brush art markers, add stamped splatters over the brayered images.

Last, add the finishing touches with a twisting spatter brush. This is a small circular brush that is dipped into calligraphy ink and twisted against an attached metal bar to make it spatter.

The results will be fantastic!

BEACH BABY

Shown on page 109.

Brayer seashells on white glossy paper to create a background. Enhance background by stamping additional seashells directly onto the page. Spatter background paper as desired.

Using rubber stamps, stamp two photo frames, several seashells, and banner on sticker paper.

Using a colored marker, write the desired phrase on the banner.

Trim two photos to fit inside stamped frames and cut out all stamped images to make stickers.

Trim remaining photo as desired. Adhere photo on coordinating color of paper and trim with wave paper edgers.

Lay-out the page and carefully adhere all photos and stamped image stickers into position on the background paper.

SANTA SULLIVAN

Shown on page 111.

Brayer poinsettias on white glossy paper to create a background. Enhance background by stamping additional poinsettias directly onto the page. Spatter background paper as desired.

Using rubber stamps, stamp rope frames, additional poinsettias, and banner on sticker paper.

Using a colored marker, write the desired phrase on the banner.

Trim photos to fit inside stamped frames and cut out all stamped images to make stickers.

Lay-out the page and carefully adhere all photos and stamped image stickers into position on the background paper.

VIRGIN ISLANDS

Shown on page 112.

Brayer tropical leaves on white glossy paper to create a background. Enhance background by stamping additional tropical leaves and flowers directly onto the page. Spatter background paper as desired.

Using rubber stamps, stamp rope frames and additional tropical flowers on sticker paper.

Trim photos to fit inside stamped frames and cut out all stamped images to make stickers. If desired, silhouette one photo.

Lay-out the page and carefully adhere all photos and stamped image stickers into position on the background paper.

SAMANTHA

Shown on page 113.

Brayer wildflowers on white glossy paper to create a background. Enhance background by stamping additional wildflowers directly onto the page. Spatter background paper as desired.

Using rubber stamps, stamp rope frames, additional wildflowers, and banner on sticker paper.

Using a colored marker, write the desired phrase on the banner.

Trim photos to fit inside stamped frames and cut out all stamped images to make stickers. If desired, silhouette one photo.

Lay-out the page and carefully adhere all photos and stamped image stickers into position on the background paper.

BEST IN THE WEST

Shown on page 114.

Brayer cowboy hats on white glossy paper to create a background. Enhance background by stamping additional cowboy hats directly onto the page. Spatter background paper as desired.

Using rubber stamps, stamp wood frames, additional cowboy hats, and award ribbon on sticker paper.

Using a colored marker, write the desired phrase in the center of the award ribbon.

Trim photos to fit inside stamped frames and cut out all stamped images to make stickers.

Lay-out the page and carefully adhere all photos and stamped image stickers into position on the background paper.

Santa Sullivan

U.S. VIRGIN ISLANDS
T·13995
RENT ME
FROM
ABC
S55
SUZUKI
U.S. VIRGIN ISLANDS
T·13995

Samantha

BEST IN THE WEST!
NOT FOR PEOPLES HORZES ONLY

Spattered Backgrounds

SOMETHING SMELLS FISHY!

With this technique, pages are instantly transformed into backgrounds with flair.

The first step is to stamp with a paint splatter design rubber stamp and white embossing powder. This technique is achieved by applying embossing ink to the rubber stamp and stamping the image onto the background paper. You may want to stamp the image two or three times, re-inking each time.

Immediately apply the embossing powder liberally. Pour the extra powder back into the container and tap the paper a few times to completely remove all the excess powder. If preferred, a small paintbrush can be used to remove stray powder.

Heat the image with an embossing heat gun, taking care not to hold the paper too close to the heat source as this can cause the paper to curl.

Repeat the process until the entire page has an even pattern.

Last, add the finishing touches with a twisting spatter brush. This is a small circular brush that is dipped into calligraphy ink and twisted against an attached metal bar to make it spatter.

SOMETHING SMELLS FISHY

Shown on page 115.

Create a background paper by using the spatter technique in embossed white with black spatters on teal paper.

Using rubber stamps, stamp and emboss rope frames with white on black paper.

Draw or stamp a caption box on sticker paper and cut.

Using a black marker, write the desired phrase in the center of the caption box.

Trim photos to fit inside stamped frames and cut out all stamped images to make stickers. If desired, silhouette one photo.

Lay out the page and care fully adhere all photos and stamped image stickers into position on the background paper.

KARA MARIE

Shown on page 117.

Create a background paper by using the spatter technique in embossed white with metallic gold spatters on black paper.

Using rubber stamps, stamp and emboss clusters of roses, vase, and flowers with white and metallic colors on black and natural paper.

Stamp and emboss banner with black on gold paper.

Using a white opaque pen, write the desired phrase on the banner. Highlight writing with a fine-tip black marker.

Trim photos as desired. Adhere photos on metallic paper and trim to a 1/4" mat.

Cut out all stamped images to make stickers.

Lay-out the page and carefully adhere all photos and stamped image stickers into position on the background paper.

NEW MEXICO

Shown on page 118.

Create a background paper by using the spatter technique in embossed white with red spatters on orange paper.

Using rubber stamps, stamp twig frames, cacti, chile peppers, and directional sign on sticker paper.

Stamp or write the desired phrase on the directional sign.

Trim two photos to fit inside stamped frames. Trim remaining photo as desired. Adhere photo on rust paper and trim with leaf pattern paper edgers.

Cut out all stamped images to make stickers.

Lay-out the page and carefully adhere all photos and stamped image stickers into position on the background paper.

KaraMarie

Josefinds
New
Mexico

Spatter Brush Streaking Backgrounds

This technique is done with a twisting spatter brush, which is a round brush with a movable knob and a rod attached that interferes with the bristles when moved into position.

Dip the brush into ink or acrylic paint and tap off excess. Pull the brush across the paper in an arc and repeat. If desired, move the rod up into the brush and turn to get a fine spatter of ink or paint overall.

Let dry thoroughly between ink colors.

We ♥ New York!

WE LOVE NEW YORK

Shown on page 119.

Create a background paper by using the streaking technique with black ink on white paper.

Using rubber stamps, stamp and emboss photo corners with white on black paper. Stamp and emboss several buildings with white on red paper.

Stamp additional buildings, marquee, and heart on sticker paper.

Using a black marker, write the desired phrase in the center of the marquee.

Trim photos as desired. Adhere photos on red paper and trim to a 1/4" mat.

Cut out all stamped images to make stickers.

Lay-out the page and carefully adhere all photos and stamped image stickers into position on the background paper.

LA MESILLA

Shown on page 121.

Create a background paper by using the streaking technique with black ink on tan paper. Lightly spatter ink.

Using rubber stamps, stamp cacti and grass on sticker paper.

Trim photos as desired. Adhere photos on black paper and trim to a 1/4" mat. If desired, silhouette one photo.

Cut out all stamped images to make stickers.

Lay-out the page and carefully adhere all photos and stamped image stickers into position on the background paper.

TUCSON, ARIZONA

Shown on page 122.

Create a background paper by using the streaking technique with black, gold, and orange ink on white paper. Allow to dry thoroughly between colors.

Using rubber stamps, stamp and emboss adobe frames with copper on black paper. Stamp and emboss cacti and pottery with white and copper ink on black paper.

Stamp banner on sticker paper.

Using a colored marker, write desired phrase on the banner.

Trim photos to fit into stamped frames and cut out all stamped images to make stickers. Adhere two photos on coordinating color of paper and trim to a 1/16" mat. Cut two frames to make into photo corners.

Lay-out the page and carefully adhere all photos and stamped image stickers into position on the background paper.

BUTTERFIELD
OVERLAND TRAIL
Overland mail stage line.
St. Louis to San Francisco
1858-1861
Forerunner to the Pony Express
OFFICIAL SCENIC HISTORIC MARKER
LA MESILLA
After the Treaty of Guadalupe Hidalgo, which concluded the Mexican War in 1848, the Mexican government commissioned Cura Ramón Ortiz to settle Mesilla. He brought families from New Mexico and from Paso del Norte (modern Ciudad Juárez) to populate the Mesilla Civil Colony Grant, which by 1850 had over 800 inhabitants.

Tucson with Jane

GALLERY OF THEMED ALBUMS

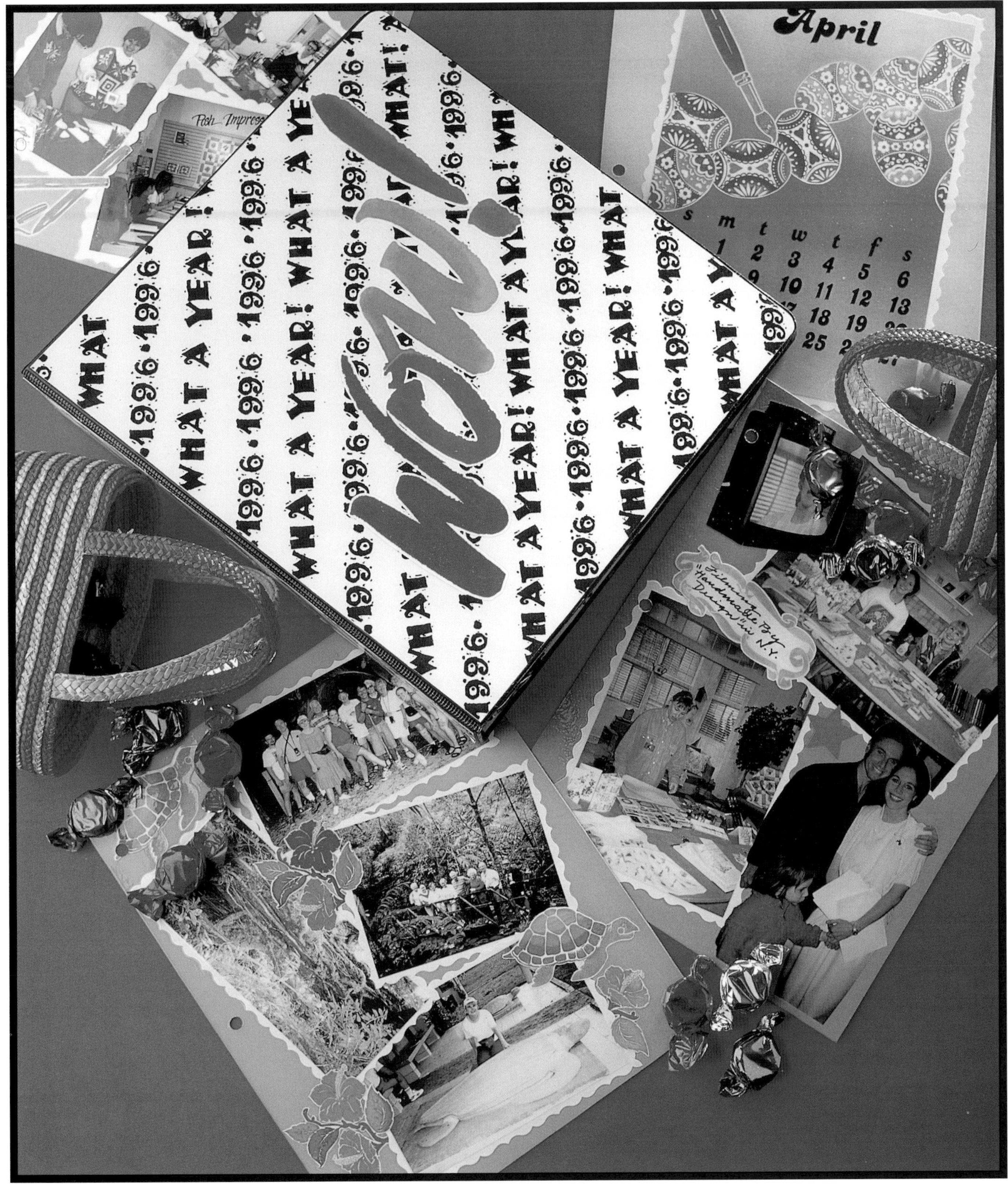

JANUARY
S M T W T F S
1 2 3 4 5 6
7 8 9 10 11 12 13
14 15 16 17 18 19 20
21 22 23 24 25 26 27
28 29 30 31
MARCH
S M T W T F S
1 2
3 4 5 6 7 8 9
10 11 12 13 14 15 16
17 18 19 20 21 22 23
24 31 25 26 27 28 29 30
May
s m t w t f s
1 2 3 4
5 6 7 8 9 10 11
12 13 14 15 16 17 18
19 20 21 22 23 24 25
26 27 28 29 30 31
Dee '96
September
s m t w t f s
1 2 3 4 5 6 7
8 9 10 11 12 13 14
15 16 17 18 19 20 21
22 23 24 25 26 27 28
29 30

THE GREAT
Rubber Stamp
BOOK
Designing
Making
Using
DEE GRUENIG
GOOD STAMPS STAMP GOODS

Celebrating.....
Hart's B'day
KOREA with the U.S. ARMY
WELCOME TO CASEY
ARTS & CRAFTS CENTER
happy birthday
hap!
Kid's Birthday Party Workshops!

Welcome
CAMP WALKER
Skills Development Training
US Army Arts and Crafts
1942 • 1992 • Serving Soldiers 50 Years
Kim Sang Son
•WON, KYU HWONG
•KIM SONG TAE
•CHONG SAN KIM
•YI, HO SON
•CHONG SAM YUNG
•KIM YUN K
•CHUNG HWAN YOM
•SANG CHON KIM
CHU YONG YUN
•JIM BRIDGES
•EMILY BEAN
•FRAN MURRAY
•NYDIA MEJIAS
Ink
Have a Great Time!
WISH I WAS THERE!
Korea '96

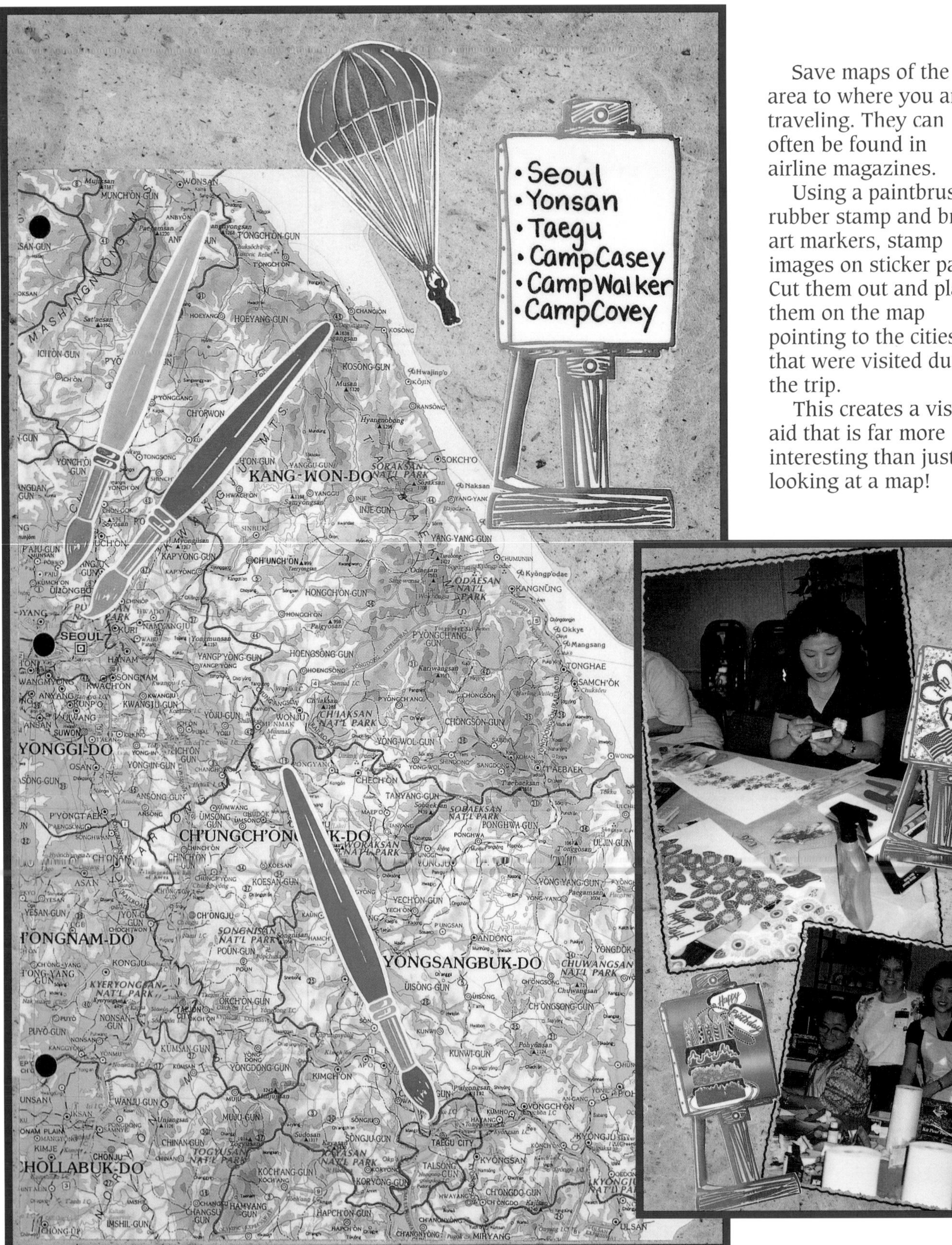

Save maps of the area to where you are traveling. They can often be found in airline magazines.

Using a paintbrush rubber stamp and brush art markers, stamp images on sticker paper. Cut them out and place them on the map pointing to the cities that were visited during the trip.

This creates a visual aid that is far more interesting than just looking at a map!

Take colorful photos. This makes it easier to color coordinate when it is time to create the album.

Color the rubber stamps with brush art markers that coordinate with the colors in the photos.

Stamp images on sticker paper. Cut them out and, if desired, overlap them onto the photo(s).

Keep mementos of your trip such as:

- airline tickets
- travel vouchers
- menus
- ticket stubs
- receipts

These can be color copied in an enlarged or reduced format to fit the area on the page in which you are working.

Unusual items, such as doilies, fabrics, and textured papers, can also be color copied and used to help preserve a memory.

MRS F C GORHAM=
:719 SOUTH CITRUS LOSA=
:BEST WISHES MANY HAPPY RETURNS OF THE DAY LOVE=
ROY USS TEXAS.
WESTERN UNION
TELEGRAM
FORGET ME NOT

White embossing on black photo safe paper creates drama for those old black and white photos.

Make color copies of the photos in black and white to remove the yellowing areas on the photos.

Instead of using a frame on these photos, draw a line around each one with a white correction pen. Leave a tiny black area around each photo.

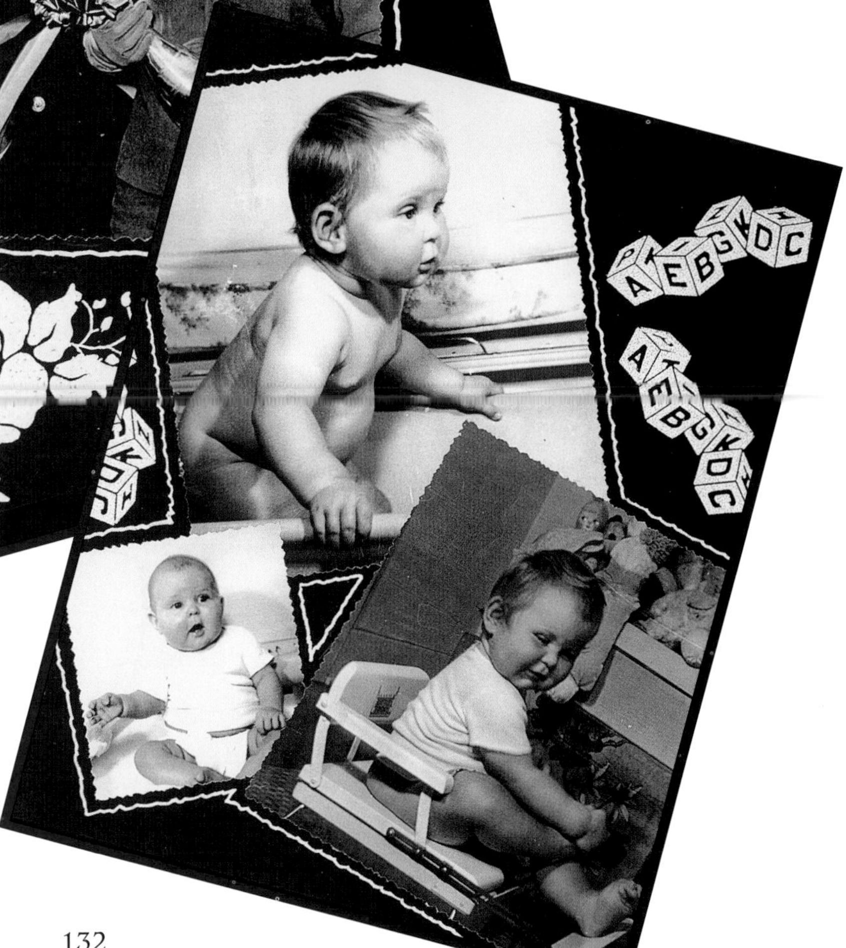

This type of theme album is a perfect gift idea. Take the old photos that your parents or grandparents have in a shoebox down in the basement and transform them into a classic, timeless work of art and beauty to be shared with family members and friends for many years to come!

WOW! WHAT A SCHOOL YEAR
1995–1996
Sun Mon Tues Wed Thurs Fri Sat
DANNY AND KRISTIE
SEPTEMBER
JULY
Rustin and Murphy... leading a dog's life!

Field Trip to Von's Aliso Viejo
A VISIT TO THE PUMPKIN PATCH
A VISIT TO DAD'S CO!!
Mon Van Moving Services
GLOBAL
GLOBAL
WORLD WIDE MOVING
ARDMORE
ACES
ADMIT ONE
TENNIS LESSONS
ADMIT ONE

DANNY'S CLASS
Miss Miller's Classroom 3rd Grade
No. 2
Miss Miller 1·9·9·5 First Day of School

COSTA RICA
WHOLE ROAST BEAN
10 OZ
AFRICAN
COFFEE

Sarchi's great Butterfly Farm!

Woke up
to the
beautiful
sights of
San Jose - So
green, lush
and clean!
The taxi that
picked us up
took us on a great ride from
San Jose to Escazú. The
countryside was beautiful
so green with beautiful
flowers everywhere. Saw a
goat on a leash! Friendly
people everywhere. Garbage is
kept in an elevated box in front
of each house. Went by the
lovely Embassy's - including
the big US Embassy! Came to
deep in a lovely bed & breakfast
There were the Lahrs, Darle
and the five Pierces! What
unbelievable fun to see
everyone again!

A Trip to Lake Tahoe
Fabulous Fans!
HAWKS!
WOW!
WHAT A SEASON!
CALIFORNIA STATE
CHAMPIONS
GIRLS · DIVISION II
1996 · 1997
Laguna Hills High School

This sports journal, created for a very special coach, documents each and every detail of a particular basketball season.

The background papers chosen were alternated to create variety, yet were color coordinated to tie in with the theme.

The basketball paper is great, but too busy to use on every page. Therefore, coordinating prints in black and white were the perfect compliment.

Color copies of basketballs were cut out and used as stickers to enhance the pages.

The newspaper articles were color copied in a reduced format so they would fit on the page, but are still readable. The schedule and ticket stubs add information and interest and make a nice alternative to handwritten journaling.

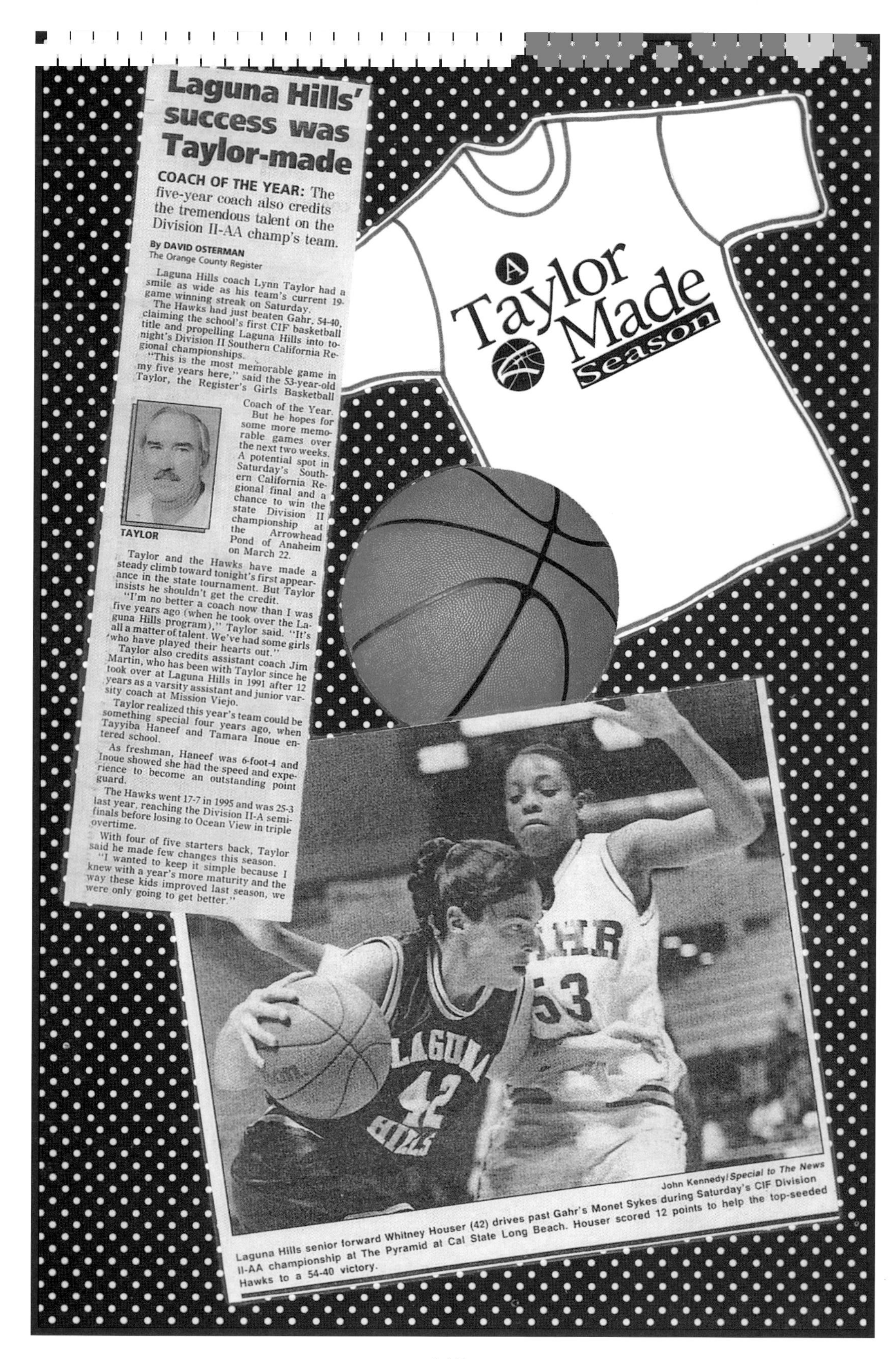

Laguna Hills' success was Taylor-made

COACH OF THE YEAR: The five-year coach also credits the tremendous talent on the Division II-AA champ's team.

By DAVID OSTERMAN
The Orange County Register

Laguna Hills coach Lynn Taylor had a smile as wide as his team's current 19-game winning streak on Saturday.

The Hawks had just beaten Gahr, 54-40, claiming the school's first CIF basketball title and propelling Laguna Hills into tonight's Division II Southern California Regional championships.

"This is the most memorable game in my five years here," said the 53-year-old Taylor, the Register's Girls Basketball Coach of the Year.

TAYLOR

But he hopes for some more memorable games over the next two weeks. A potential spot in Saturday's Southern California Regional final and a chance to win the state Division II championship at the Arrowhead Pond of Anaheim on March 22.

Taylor and the Hawks have made a steady climb toward tonight's first appearance in the state tournament. But Taylor insists he shouldn't get the credit.

"I'm no better a coach now than I was five years ago (when he took over the Laguna Hills program)," Taylor said. "It's all a matter of talent. We've had some girls who have played their hearts out."

Taylor also credits assistant coach Jim Martin, who has been with Taylor since he took over at Laguna Hills in 1991 after 12 years as a varsity assistant and junior varsity coach at Mission Viejo.

Taylor realized this year's team could be something special four years ago, when Tayyiba Haneef and Tamara Inoue entered school.

As freshman, Haneef was 6-foot-4 and Inoue showed she had the speed and experience to become an outstanding point guard.

The Hawks went 17-7 in 1995 and was 25-3 last year, reaching the Division II-A semifinals before losing to Ocean View in triple overtime.

With four of five starters back, Taylor said he made few changes this season.

"I wanted to keep it simple because I knew with a year's more maturity and the way these kids improved last season, we were only going to get better."

John Kennedy/*Special to The News*

Laguna Hills senior forward Whitney Houser (42) drives past Gahr's Monet Sykes during Saturday's CIF Division II-AA championship at The Pyramid at Cal State Long Beach. Houser scored 12 points to help the top-seeded Hawks to a 54-40 victory.

INDEX

A SPECIAL DAY 52, 54
AIR SHOW 64, 66
ALASKA 89-90
ALOHA! 26, 29
ALVA LOUISE 32-33
BACKYARD SUMMER DAYS 76, 78
BANDANAS 82, 84
BANGKOK 68, 70
BE ALL THAT
YOU CAN BE! 90, 92
BEACH BABY 109-110
BEACH BUDDIES 106, 108
BEACH COMBING 44, 46
BEACH PARTY 93-94
BEAR & ME 48, 50
BEST IN THE WEST 110, 114
BIG CHIEF 40-41
BIRTHDAY KING 68, 70
BORDER STAMPING
BACKGROUNDS 39-42
BOUNTIFUL HARVEST 90-91
BRAYERED IMAGE
BACKGROUNDS 85-88
BRAYERED LANDSCAPES 89-92
BRAYERED PEN DESIGNS 71-74
BRAYERED PLAID AND
GINGHAMS 75-80
BRAYERED RAINBOW PAD
BACKGROUND 93-96
BRAYERED RAINBOW PAD
RESIST BACKGROUNDS 101-104
BRAYERED RAINBOW PAD
WITH SHADOWS
AND HIGHLIGHTS 97-100
BRAYERED REVERSE
WITH SPATTERS 109-114
BRAYERS & SPONGES 9-10
BRIDGE CROSSING 102, 104
CAMELOT WEDDING 16, 18
CANNON'S CHRISTMAS 40, 42
CARIBBEAN FUN 15-16
CHINA 51-52
COACH OF THE YEAR 56, 58
COLORFUL SRI LANKA 68-69
COMPRESSED SPONGE
BACKGROUND 25-30
COPIED PAPER
BACKGROUNDS 31-34
COSTA RICA 16, 18, 106, 108
CREATING ALBUMS
WITH THEMES 12, 123-143
DADDY'S DAY 81-82
DADDY'S HOME 5, 56
DEE & WARREN 32, 34
DODGERS BASEBALL 94, 96
DOUG & CAREY 40, 42
EASTER MORNING 94-95
EAT YOUR VEGGIES 44-45
EGYPT 31-32
ELEPHANTS 67-68
EMBOSSING POWDERS &
HEAT TOOL 10
ENGINE ENGINE
NUMBER NINE 22, 24
ENHANCED BRAYERED
BACKGROUNDS 81-84
FABRIC COPIED
BACKGROUND 35-38
FABULOUS FRIENDS 36-37
FEEDING THE HORSES 72, 74
FOURTH OF JULY 52, 54
FRESH STRAWBERRIES 85-86
FULL PATTERN
BACKGROUNDS 47-50
FUTURE BASEBALL
STARS 20, 22-23
GALLERY OF
THEMED ALBUMS 123-143
GRAMPA'S GIRL 75-76
HAITI 35-36
HAM BROTHERS 55-56
HIP HIP HOORAY 102-103
HOME ON THE RANGE 106-107
HONG KONG 36, 38
HOWDY PARTNER 22-23
HUGS & KISSES 71-72
INDIANS 98, 100
ITALIAN GOURMET 36, 38
JAKE'S & COLBY'S GARDEN 48-49
JUICY, JUICY, JUICY 86, 88
KARA MARIE 116-117
KEEPING A JOURNAL
OF SPECIAL EVENTS 13, 140
LA MESILLA 120-121
LADYBUGS & IVY 76, 79
LAS VEGAS! 56-57
LITTLE ARTIST 16-17
LITTLE INDIANS 72, 74
LUAU LAUGHTER 47-48
LUNCH ON THE BEACH 64, 66
MACHU PICCHU 32, 34
MARKERS & PENS 8-9
METALLIC EMBOSSED
FRAMES 67-70
METRIC CONVERSION CHART 14
MICHAEL 40, 42
MONTANA 76-77
MY BABY BOY 28-29
NEW MEXICO 116, 118
NEW YEAR'S EVE 48, 50
PANSY PORTRAIT 20-21
PAR-FECT DAY 59-60
PEN STRIPE
BACKGROUND 19-24
PIRATE PARTY 72, 74
PLAY BALL 97-98
PLAYER OF THE GAME 20, 23
PLAYGROUND PASTIME 26, 28-29
PUMPKIN PATCH 86-87
RILEY 82-83
RUBBER STAMPS 8-9
SAILING AWAY 40, 42
SAMANTHA 110, 113
SANTA SULLIVAN 110-111
SEA WORLD 43-44
SET SAIL FROM AMERICA 28, 30
SEVEN STEPS TO ALBUM
ART SUCCESS 12
SHADES OF GRAY
BACKGROUNDS 43-46
SIMPLY PAPER AND
FRAMES 15-18
SOMETHING SMELLS FISHY 115-116
SPATTER BRUSH STREAKING
BACKGROUNDS 119-122
SPATTERED
BACKGROUNDS 115-118
SPONGE BRAYER WATERCOLOR
BACKGROUNDS 105-108
SPRING HAS SPRUNG 105-106
SPRING WEDDING 1, 44
SRI LANKA 25-26
STAMP PADS 8-9
STAMPED LANDSCAPE
BACKGROUNDS 59-62
STAMPED NEWSPAPER
BACKGROUND 55-58
STICKER PAPERS 9-10
SUDAN 26-27
SUMMER DAYS 60-61
SUNFLOWER BABY 19-20
SWEET AS A ROSE 98-99
TROPICAL PARADISE 101-102
TUCSON, ARIZONA 120, 122
UNDER THE SEA 28-29
UNDERWATER ADVENTURE 64-65
USING COLOR COPIED
PHOTOS 10-11
USING STICKER PAPER
FRAMES 11
VACATION FUN 39-40
VENEZUELA 60, 62
VIRGIN ISLANDS 110, 112
WANTED 76, 80
WARREN SKYDIVES 52-53
WE LOVE NEW YORK 119-120
WE LOVE YOU SANTA 52, 54
WELCOME TO
NEW MEXICO 22-23
WHITE EMBOSSED FRAMES 63-66
WHITE PATTERN
BACKGROUNDS 51-54
WINTER FUN 63-64
ZION NATIONAL PARK 72-73